# REPORT
## OF THE
# COMMITTEE
## ON THE OPERATION OF THE
# SEXUAL
# CONTAINMENT
# ACT

Chairman: Michael Schofield

*Presented to Parliament by the Secretary of State for the Home Department, the Secretary of State for Scotland and the Secretary of State for Wales by Command of Her Majesty, October 1984*

*LONDON*
DAVIS-POYNTER LIMITED

CMND. 9989

First published in 1978 by
Davis-Poynter Ltd
20 Garrick Street London WC2E 9BJ

ISBN 0 7067 0223 9

Printed in Great Britain by Bristol Typesetting Co. Ltd,
Barton Manor St Philips Bristol

# REPORT OF THE COMMITTEE ON THE OPERATION OF THE SEXUAL CONTAINMENT ACT

*Members of the Committee*

MR MICHAEL SCHOFIELD, MA *(Chairman)*

MR LEOPOLD BLOOM, MP

THE REVD CANON FREDERICK CHASUBLE, DD

SIR GEORGE CROFTS, KCMG, OBE

PROFESSOR JIM DIXON, CBE, DLitt, FBA, FSA, FRHistS, FRSL

MISS FRANCES HILL, SRN, MTD, FHA

MR OLIVER MELLORS, JP

* MR TOM PARSONS, OBE

MR JAMES PORTER, QC, MP

† MRS WINSTON SMITH

DR O. SPIELVOGEL, MB, CHB, FRCPE, FRCPsych, DPM, FRSE

## Secretaries

MR BRYN ELLIS

MR ANTHONY SKYRME

* Resigned April 1984
† Appointed May 1984

# Contents

*Appendix A    Technical and Anatomical Problems*

Brief Resumé of Possible Male Recording Devices
The Development of the Orgasm Recording Device
The Development of a Female Orgasm Recording Device

*Appendix B    Case Histories*

*Appendix C    Evidence Submitted by SIFS*

# Foreword

To:
The Secretary of State for the Home Department
The Secretary of State for Scotland
The Secretary of State for Wales

1. The Committee was appointed in February 1984 with the following terms of reference:

'To review the operation of the Sexual Containment Act 1981, to make recommendations and to report within six months.'

2. The Committee held 12 meetings totalling 16 days including two three-day meetings, one of which was held at St Andrews and the other in Majorca.

3. The requirement to report within six months made it impossible to commission any long term research, but we were able to arrange for the Office of Population Censuses and Surveys to carry out a small survey of subjects who had experienced particular problems under the Act; this research report included a number of case histories of people who felt especially aggrieved. We have tried to disentangle the different elements in the problems, but we have not been able to provide definitive answers to all the questions which were raised.

4. The members of the Committee desire to express their gratitude for the amount of time spent and trouble taken by all those who submitted memoranda, wrote letters and gave oral evidence. We received evidence from 30 organizations, and 17 individuals. We heard evidence from 13 organizations represented by 21 witnesses who attended meetings of the Committee. We have studied numerous books and articles, surveys and opinion polls; we refer to some of these in the footnotes.

5. We have divided the report into four parts and have added three appendices. Part I of our report was written by officials in the Home Office, who were advising us on the history and development of sexual containment. Parts II, III and IV were written by

the Chairman. Appendix A contains the technical details, which we suggest should be read in conjunction with Part I by those who are unfamiliar with the basic provisions of the Act. In Appendix B we have included some extracts from the transcripts of tapes recorded during our commissioned survey because we felt it was important that room be found in this report for people to express their views in their own words. The reasons for adding an extract from the SIF Society's evidence in Appendix C are explained in Part III of our report.

6. We should like to take this opportunity to put on record our thanks to Mr Bryn Ellis and Mr Anthony Skyrme, who have given us considerable assistance in every possible way.

# PART I

# HISTORY AND DEVELOPMENT

## The Background

7. Many foreign countries have made enquiries about the operation of the Sexual Containment Act. In South America and in other countries where the influence of the Roman Catholic Church still persists, considerable interest has been shown in this great experiment. Should this undertaking prove to be a success, it is not only the idea but also the actual mechanisms that can be exported and we can hopefully expect orders running into several million pounds. Accordingly we thought it would be appropriate to sketch in the historical background for the sake of those who have not had the privilege of living through this experience.

8. The origins of this experiment can be traced back to the heyday of what used to be called the permissive society. For many years concern had been expressed about the moral standards of the young. In time it became obvious that this concupiscence had spread to all ages and most social classes. There were signs, although it is always difficult to get precise evidence, that sexual licentiousness was affecting other facets of the British way of life. Many speakers reminded us of the collapse of the Roman Empire and suggested that we were about to suffer a similar fate. Letters to *The Times* frequently suggested that London was no better than a cesspool and there were references to Rabelaisian celebrations in the parks.

9. Although the moral objections were uppermost, there were also strong economic reasons for controlling excessive sexual activities. Since 1950 Great Britain had endured many economic crises with the result that cause and effect had become confused. At first it was thought that the recession of 1975-8 had been caused by inflation and unrestrained wage demands, but it is now believed

that a major cause of the disaster was the sexual intemperance of the work force.

10. The Arts Council supplied cultural evidence to support the economic arguments. Unencumbered artistic expression in the performing arts was said to be the direct result of free sexual expression. Although we have heard other arguments that challenge this view, it cannot be denied that the arts have become more disciplined since the operation of the Sexual Containment Act. For example, most paintings are representational today; plays have a beginning, middle and usually a happy ending; classical ballet and opera revivals are now very popular, usually a sign of artistic order and discipline.

11. Concern about the low productivity of the British worker and the anarchical products of the British artist has led to a revival of the Freudian concept of sublimation. It will be remembered that this was the idea that when the individual reduced the number of sexual acts, the energy he conserved as a result of this restraint would be diverted into other activities.[1] So with less sex the worker would produce more and the artist would become more disciplined. The validity of this concept may not appear immediately obvious after a close study of the sex lives of certain very well-known artists. But it must be recognized that when we speak about people like Chopin, Picasso, Shakespeare and other famous artists of that calibre, we are talking about genius, which is an exception to all rules. However, it was confidently expected that second-rank painters, writers and performers would benefit from sublimation.

12. When the pill and other contraceptives became available on the National Health Service, it was possible for the first time to separate sex for pleasure from sex for reproduction. Unfortunately girls still had unwanted pregnancies and the medical profession was slow to provide out-patient abortion clinics. Nevertheless the risks of sexual intercourse were gradually being reduced. Only the venereal diseases continued to provide a useful, albeit capricious, curb on uncontrolled libertinism.

---

[1] Freud, S., (*Three Essays on the Theory of Sexuality*, Imago, 1949) was not quite so specific as this, but his followers have clarified and restated the original concept – see Ruitenbeek, H. M. (Ed.), *Psychoanalysis and Female Sexuality*, University Press, 1966.

13. So much emphasis had been laid on preventing promiscuity among young unmarried men and women that the sexual behaviour of married couples had escaped the notice of the moral authorities. A reasonable amount of sexual intercourse between man and wife is to be expected, but there are limits and there was considerable evidence to show that many people were exceeding these limits. As sexual intercourse became less risky, people felt inclined to indulge more often. This was particularly the case with married couples because their partner was readily available. There were reports of multitudinous sex acts which would be unbelievable had they not been authenticated by university sociologists.

14. If people spend too much time indulging in sexual intercourse and even more time thinking about it, other parts of our national life are bound to suffer. It was said that our failure to win the World Cup, the Ryder Cup, the Davis Cup and the Ashes were all examples of this. It was also said in those days that television had ruined our taste for good conversation and an active social life, but it is now believed that it was not only TV which had made us home-bound and lackadaisical. Excessive sexual activities seemed to have weakened our national resolve.

15. There was also an important psychological problem; the gravity of this was not fully appreciated at the time, but in retrospect it is now realized that the loyalty of the British working man was being severely strained. It was not so well understood in those days that it was the women who wanted to have more sex and it was the men who were finding it difficult to meet the extra demands that were being made on them. Consequently there was a growing campaign for sexual restraint. Although a few women were active in this campaign, it was mostly men who were loudly sounding the alarm about the dangers of too much sex. In most cases the speakers urged sexual restraint for moral reasons, but later research has shown that those who were most prominent in this campaign tended to be married men who were finding it difficult to satisfy the sexual desires of their wives. In practice the campaign was publicised as an appeal for the protection of women, but in reality it was the men who felt in need of protection.

16. What these men really wanted was some sort of restriction on the number of sex acts in a week or a month, but at that time

it was not clear how this could be done. The best hope seemed to be to limit all forms of sexual stimulation. The main platforms in the campaign were for increased censorship and a demand 'to reinforce the dikes against obscenity'.[2]

17. The much-publicised Longford report on pornography urged the adoption of a law which would punish the publication of material whose effect 'is to outrage contemporary standards of decency or humanity accepted by the public at large.'[3] This recommendation was expressly rejected by the Home Secretary of the Conservative government then in power, but the judges decided that since Common Law already contained the power to punish outrages to contemporary standards of decency, it was an offence to write or sell publications which shock ordinary members of the public without the necessity of having to prove that they had a corrupting influence.[4] Thus the chief recommendation of the *Longford Report* was implemented, perhaps not by a parliamentary majority, but by the decision of three out of five judges sitting in the House of Lords.

18. The judges also decided to make more use of the 'conspiracy to corrupt public morals', a doctrine based on a statement made in 1774 by Lord Mansfield who asserted: 'Whatever is against good morality and decency, the principles of our law prohibit and the King's Court as the general censor and guardian of the public morals is bound to restrain and punish.'[5] For many years the judges did not appreciate that this doctrine placed a duty upon them to punish miscreants who would otherwise have escaped because their actions were not strictly illegal. But in 1961 the House of Lords arrogated to the British judiciary the task of serving as custodians of the nation's morals to 'guard the moral welfare of the State against attacks which may be more insidious because they are novel and unprepared for.' Now it is accepted that judges have a residual power to declare illegal all the 'ways in which the wickedness of men may disrupt society.'[6]

19. The judges were also able to diminish the unfortunate effects

---

[2] These are the words used by ex-President Nixon in one of his frequent messages to Congress against obscene language.
[3] Page 383 of *Pornography – The Longford Report*, Coronet Books, 1972.
[4] *Knullar Ltd. v DPP* (1972), 2 All ER 898.
[5] *Jones v Randall* (1774), 1 Cowp 17.
[6] *Shaw v DPP* (1961), All ER 446.

of the 1967 Sexual Offences Act by introducing the concept that some legal acts are less legal than others. The view expressed by the court[7] was that this Act had made homosexual conduct 'merely exempted from criminal penalties' but did not make it 'lawful in the full sense.'

20. It must not be thought that Parliament was prepared to stand by and watch the judiciary usurp its sovereignty. Several Bills were introduced into the House of Commons which also dealt with moral matters. The most important was the Act which abolished the distinction between public exhibitions and private clubs, skilfully drafted so that an individual's sexual behaviour in the privacy of his home can now be brought within the ambit of the law.

21. Unfortunately these enactments, pronouncements and warnings were not as effective as had been hoped despite the work put in by ministers, judges, churchmen and other moral authorities. Premarital sexual intercourse was still widespread despite attempts to introduce legal and psychological hazards, while married couples still continued to have sex whenever they felt so inclined.

22. The Prime Minister and the Archbishop of York[8] took part in a TV Special broadcast on all networks at a peak viewing time. The programme also contained a specially written Papal Encyclical and a series of filmed interviews with inmates who recounted their unfortunate experiences as a result of excessive sexual activities. Although this programme was repeated many times, no noticeable change in sexual habits could be detected in the general population, except that there was a tendency for those who had previously had very little sex to have none at all after seeing the programme. But those who had high sexual frequencies did not appear to be impressed either by the moral arguments, explicit warnings, or direct threats.

23. The Trades Union Congress suggested that there should be a loosely-worded undertaking between men and women promising not to make excessive demands upon each other. The 'Sexual Contract', as it was called, received a lot of publicity, but in the end the government were forced to conclude that voluntary restraint was

---

[7] House of Lords, 15 June 1972
[8] For various reasons the recently appointed Archbishop of Canterbury was unavailable.

not going to work and some form of statutory control would be needed.

24. A delegation of senior members of Parliament was sent to China to see if any of their methods could usefully be applied to this country. The Chinese have an enviable record. Rates for illegitimacy and venereal disease have fallen dramatically, and the prevalence of premarital sexual intercourse is said to have gone down while the age at which couples get married has gone up – a remarkable achievement.

25. When the delegation returned, after some delay due to a misunderstanding about the motives of one of the members during a visit to one of the schools for retraining promiscuous girls, it reported that it would be very expensive to set up the camps for thought-control and it would take time to build up the elaborate network of informers necessary for the adequate supervision of private sexual behaviour. Romantic love is discouraged in China as all love must be lavished on the Chairman.[9] The delegation was uncertain whether the Queen would be the most suitable equivalent in this country and Sir Harold Wilson, in a minority report, suggested that an ex-Prime Minister might be a more appropriate recipient of national love.

26. It was recognized that the ideal would be a change of attitude backed by sanctions, but it was believed that a strategic plan based on this ideal would not be possible in this country. British attitudes are notoriously difficult to change even on matters such as food, sport, or political allegiance. Sociologists were of the opinion that it would take several decades to alter attitudes to sex.[10] The problem was urgent. It was believed that a solution which involved

---

[9] 'Love between man and woman is a psychosomatic activity which consumes energy and wastes time. On the other hand, love of the Chairman takes no time at all, and is in itself a powerful tonic' – *The Peking Workers' Daily.*

[10] 'Since most of the sexual orientations of the adult personality are results of events that are not reversible through conventional means, there are no grounds for predicting that the sexual life can be easily changed. Given our difficulties in changing behaviour of schizophrenics, drug addicts or juvenile delinquents, or even of changing the political party affiliation of others, there seems to be a curious contradiction in the belief that sexual behaviour is immediately amenable to change from the slightest external impulse.' Gagnon, John, 'Sexuality and Sexual Learning', *Journal of the Study of Interpersonal Processes,* 28:3 212–28, 1965.

a gradual change of opinion would not be in time to prevent the impending debacle. The concensus among moral authorities was that some kind of physical control would have to be applied.

## The American Contribution

27. A few years earlier various scientists in America had become interested in the idea of attaching some form of mechanism to the human body that would act as a physical control over sexual activities. Various ideas were tried out on volunteers, but none of them were entirely satisfactory either because they were too cumbersome or because they were unsafe. Although the object was to limit the number of sexual acts, it was thought that a machine that required the users to adopt an unfamiliar position or which over-heated during intercourse would not be acceptable.

28. The original intention, indeed the very strong motivation behind the hundreds of hours of scientific endeavour, was to find some solution to the problem of over-population in the developing countries. By then it was recognized that birth control was going to make only a marginal difference to the rate of population growth. Indeed it had become clear at the first United Nations World Population Conference in Budapest in 1974 that many countries had rejected the neo-Malthusian approach put forward by the developed Western countries that birth control was a prerequisite to solving the problems of the Third World.

29. The government of the United States was becoming increasingly alarmed at the ominous situation created by the increase in the population of the developing countries. Millions of dollars were made available to scientists in an attempt to find a solution to this threat. The population of the developed countries was not increasing and could not be increased if the inhabitants were to continue to enjoy their present standard of living. If the differential between Western civilization and the Third World was to be maintained, the rulers of the developing countries must be provided with the physical means of preventing over-population.

30. Unfortunately very few of the governments in African or Asian countries displayed much understanding of this scheme. Congressmen were inclined to think that most of this opposition was due to irrational anti-Americanism, inflamed by communist propa-

ganda, for they sincerely believed that it was in the best interests of the developing countries to control sexual reproduction if only they would take the long term point of view. Further efforts to correct these misunderstandings had to be abandoned when a senator introduced into Congress a special law, which in effect meant that no country would receive economic aid unless it promised to introduce some form of physical control over sex acts. This action was rather premature, if only because no satisfactory mechanism had been put on the market at that time.

31. Despite this setback, the US government continues to make funds available to medical scientists in the hope that in the course of time the developing countries will come to understand why a measure of sexual control is in their own best interests. Failing that, the use of force has not been ruled out, although the President has given an undertaking that he will take no action without first informing the UN Security Council.

## British Enterprise

32. Meanwhile similar work was proceeding in this country and it gives us considerable satisfaction to report that this has been another example, like penicillin and the jet engine, of the British genius for invention. The pioneering work and testing was done in government laboratories, the assembly work at ordnance factories, and all components, down to the last screw, have been manufactured in Britain. When the time comes to write the exciting story of the development of ORD, all of us shall be proud that we are British.

33. Such a tremendous achievement could not, of course, have been accomplished without some cost. The various prototypes had to be tested and volunteers from prisons and mental hospitals were recruited to try them out. As so often happens in the pursuit of knowledge, there were a number of unavoidable accidents. We feel it is right and proper, even in a report of this nature, that space be found to pay tribute to the many people who suffered. Without their sacrifice we should not have achieved the high level of control that we enjoy today and this report could never have been written.

34. The technical details are given in Appendix A and readers who are unfamiliar with the operations of ORD are advised to

read this.[11] In this part of the report we simply give the basic information in layman's language.

35. The orgasm recording device, better known as ORD, comes in two models. The male version 3.2 cm long, 1.8 cm wide and 0.7 cm thick. It is covered in specially developed blue[12] foam plastic and fits neatly on the perineum, the area between the scrotum and the anus. Its operation is based on the principle that there is a marked swelling of the urethral bulb[13] immediately before orgasm. ORD is sensitive to this distension and this makes it possible to record orgasms whatever may be the reason, whether it be sexual intercourse, inceptive activities,[14] masturbation or nocturnal emmissions.

36. The female ORD consists of a small circular reactor with a hole in the middle that fits over the nipple on the breast. There is a thin lead connecting the reactor to the recording mechanism which is fitted under the breast. The female ORD is larger than the male version and is fully-fashioned in order to improve the fitting qualities.[15] The overall length is 4.1 cm and the diameter is 1.5 cm. It is also padded in foam plastic coloured in a tasteful pink.

37. When the female becomes sexually excited, the areola[16] expands to more than twice its size and then contracts very rapidly immediately she experiences orgasm. This tumescence and detumescence of the areola is recorded in ORD on an electrographic tracing. As the areolar reaction occurs in both breasts, it is only necessary to wear one ORD, usually on the breast on the right. When the tracing is removed from ORD and examined in a magnified reader, the number of orgasms can be counted without difficulty. Like the male model, the female ORD records all orgasms whether they are the result of sexual intercourse, inceptive

---

[11] For example, foreigners, old age pensioners and others who are exempt.
[12] The male ORD (Mark I) was red and the female ORD (Mark I) was a darker shade of pink. Anyone found wearing these older models should be reported to the Inspectorate.
[13] For the location of the urethral bulb see the diagrams in Appendix A.
[14] Inceptive activities are defined as extensive sexual intimacies which do not involve penetration – see Schofield, Michael, *The Sexual Behaviour of Young People*, Longmans, 1965.
[15] It can best be described as roughly the shape of a miniature banana.
[16] The areola is the ring of darkened tissue on the breast surrounding the nipple. See the diagrams in Appendix A.

B

activities, masturbation with the hand or with mechanical aids.

## The American Contribution

38. It quickly became apparent to the older and more experienced members of the establishment that here was the means by which the physical control of sex could be introduced. Naturally they would have preferred a machine that would actually prevent an orgasm, or an erection, but on this occasion medical science was unable to satisfy political demands. Even so, it was clear that a satisfactory measure of control could be obtained by making it compulsory to wear ORD at all times, and by limiting by statute the number of orgasms permitted in a year.

39. It is important to realize the essential difference between the American concept and the introduction of ORD in the United Kingdom. In the former case the countries of Africa and Asia were resisting sexual control imposed from outside, but we were controlling ourselves, an altogether more acceptable state of affairs. In any case, there were many good reasons for doing so, as the more perspicacious soon realized when official government press releases and broadcasts repeated the persuasive arguments for introducing ORD.

40. The Home Secretary argued that the commercial exploitation of sex would become unprofitable after it had become compulsory to wear ORD: The strip clubs, the blue film societies and the hard porn bookshops would go out of business because the purveyors of sexual stimulation would find that people avoided these places for fear that they might be excited to the point of orgasm and this would be recorded by ORD.[17]

41. Although it was not possible to claim that ORD would immediately suppress all adultery, the repercussions were likely to be counteractive. For example, it would be quite difficult for an unfaithful husband to satisfy both a mistress and a wife with the limited number of orgasms permitted in a month. Similarly it was

---

[17] In the event the purveyors of hard pornography were able to prosper even after the introduction of ORD. Home Office officials had failed to realize that many men derive some erotic pleasure from pornography without necessarily having to seek orgasmic relief. Further legislation was required to close the bookshops and private clubs.

not expected that ORD would actually prevent premarital sexual intercourse, but it would certainly impede the promiscuous activities of the young.

42. ORD would encourage sublimation and leave more time for other things. The free indulgence in sexual intercourse without the restraining influence of the fear of pregnancy had meant that people were spending most of their leisure hours at home, which was bad business for theatres, film distributors, public houses and amusement arcades. It was not surprising, therefore, that the government received considerable support from the leisure industries in the propaganda campaign prior to the launching of ORD.

43. In the years before ORD was introduced, public opinion polls continued to report that more than 80 per cent did not approve of this increase in sexual activities at home. It is a well-proven sociological fact that private acts and public opinions do not often coincide. It is an over-simplification to conclude from this that people are very hypocritical. The government's interpretation of these public opinion polls was that unconsciously the people were asking for guidance. We are inclined to agree with this interpretation. Just as people traditionally seek an authoritative leader to guide them at times of political stress, so in times of sexual turmoil they invariably turn to the government for leadership. As the Bishop of Bath and Wells said in the House of Lords during the debate on ORD, 'If one leaves a steep precipice unfenced, many will approach the edge and some will fall; but if one erects a fence of barbed-wire, few will be malcontent and none will fall.' Most people are inwardly grateful when they are helped to avoid temptations in their private life.

44. The government's introductory campaign was supported by three active pressure groups, who helped to sway public opinion. The Categorical Society was formed in order to inculcate responsible attitudes in the young. The oddly named Carnival of White had less specific objectives but attracted public attention by arranging for entertainers (pop singers, TV pundits etc) to make declamatory speeches at large rallies. The third pressure group, the National Scopophilic Association, was led to very great effect by Mrs Mary Lighthead, the wife of a clergyman in the Midlands; in the early days she was thought of as little more than a laughing stock, but

as she learnt to present herself on TV and to make good use of the press, she became quite influential. She was often to be seen in the company of obsequious television executives at meetings and public dinners.

45. Meanwhile government spokesmen emphasized that this was not a ban on sex; it was merely a recording instrument which would aid restraint. To help people to understand, ORD was promoted with the slogan: LESS SEX BUT NOT SEXLESS.

## Statutory Regulations

46. It is unlikely that a majority was actually in favour of the introduction of ORD at that time, but the government believed that their arguments were sufficiently convincing and the situation was so urgent that it was necessary to act straight away before the issues were clouded by too much discussion. Fortunately Parliament had not found time to revoke the State of Emergency, which had been proclaimed to deal with the serious political crisis of the previous year. This enabled the government to promulgate all the necessary regulations by the use of Statutory Instruments.

47. The main provisions of the regulations are well known and as they were later incorporated with only a few amendments into the Sexual Containment Act 1981, it will not be necessary to give more than a brief summary.

48. A network of centres, known as Inspectorates, was set up to service every area of the country. Each Inspectorate was to be staffed by one Inspector, up to seven Referendaries and auxiliary personnel.

49. All persons over the age of 15 and below the age of 76, including aliens and visitors, had to report to the Inspectorate when they received a card from the National Computer. At the Inspectorate they would have ORD fitted and the regulations explained to them. Inspectors were not empowered to grant exemption.

50. Although a few subjects were uneasy at the start, they soon become accustomed to wearing the device. Every quarterly period the National Computer would send instructions to all persons offering a choice of three dates on which they were to report to the

Inspectorate, where ORD could be serviced and the number of orgasms audited.

51. The maximum number of permitted orgasms in each thirteen-week period was to be 27 for those aged 16–65 and 13[18] for those aged 66–75. Men and women over the age of 76 are allowed an unlimited number of orgasms.

52. Naturally most of the early discussion was about the permitted number of orgasms (PNO). In all new legislation which has to express a maximum quantity (eg the breathalyser), an arbitrary standard has to be chosen. It is inevitable that this will be followed immediately by criticism; some will think the number should be higher and others will maintain that it should be lower. In order to forestall this kind of criticism, the Home Office published the calculations upon which these figures were based. After lengthy consultations with churchmen, psychiatrists and other moral authorities, it was adjudged that the basic standard should be two orgasms a week with an extra one each quarter to allow for accidents.

| | | |
|---|---|---:|
| 2 orgasms a week plus 1 for 13 weeks | = | 27 |
| 27 orgasms a quarter for 1 year | = | 108 |
| 108 orgasms a year for 50 years (aged 16–65) | = | 5,400 |
| 54 orgasms a year for 10 years (aged 66–75) | = | 540 |
| Total permitted number of orgasms (PNO) | = | 5,940 |

53. To a young man or woman these regulations may seem restrictive, but taking the overall view, and the government of the day must always do this, this allowance is not ungenerous.

**The Reasons for the Delay**

54. It was possible to start fitting ORDs as soon as the regulations had been promulgated because the government had been secretly stockpiling during the previous few months, confident that the arguments in favour of ORD would prevail. Although this subterfuge was criticized at the time, we feel that it is no more than the normal provident calculation that governments can be expected to take when questions of security arise.

---

[18] 14 in each of the two winter quarterly periods.

55. Fittings started in the south-west regions of England and proceeded northwards as quickly as Inspectorates could be established. During the course of the next few weeks there were questions from members of Parliament with northern constituencies who, quite reasonably, asked why Scotland should be the last to receive these benefits. The Secretary of State for Scotland was obliged to prevaricate for a period of time, but under persistent questioning the Minister of State at the Home Office disclosed that the problem was less urgent in Scotland because behavioral studies had revealed that Scotsmen tended to have sexual intercourse less often than their counterparts in England and Wales.[19] This caused considerable indignation and Scottish Nationalists demanded an apology for the slur cast on the manhood of all Scots. Eventually the Home Secretary was obliged to admit that these research results may have been misleading.

56. Counties in the north of England also protested for similar reasons and they supported their protests with statistics to show that there was more rape, incest and indecent assault in their areas than in the south. However, the Minister of State for Home Affairs repeatedly assured them that the fitting of ORD was proceeding so well that it would only be a matter of weeks before Inspectorates were set up in the north.

57. Unfortunately the Minister's timetable proved to be over-optimistic. This was partly due to the inaccuracy of the population figures supplied by the OPCS, especially in the Midlands where large numbers of the immigrant population had for various reasons failed to register when the National Computer was first established. One of the leaders of the Pakistani community in this country said that he had no serious objection to the fundamental intentions behind the introduction of ORD, but he added: 'This is only one of a series of regulations that are threatening to regiment our people and are forcing us to adopt facets of the British way of life which we are regarding as inferior to and less civilized than our own culture.'

58. Delay was also caused by the attitude of the British Medical Association, who once again threatened to advise their members to

19 It was found that Scotswomen were not significantly different from other women.

withdraw their services from the National Health Service if ORD was fitted by non-medical personnel. This demand confused both the authorities and the public. For years doctors had been proclaiming vociferously that they were grossly overworked and had to put in many hours of overtime in order to see all their patients. Now the medical men were demanding that they should be given more work. The government was quite prepared for the doctors to take over the fitting of ORD as part of the NHS, especially as independent investigations had shown that general practitioners were not so busy as they claimed to be. Of course the BMA made it clear that doctors would require extra payment if they were to undertake this work, but after prolonged negotiations at the Department of Health and Social Security had broken down, the government announced that it would go ahead with the plan to recruit a corps of Inspectors and Referendaries to staff the new centres.

59. But the main cause of the delay was a spirited campaign of demonstrations, strikes and protest meetings once the true significance of ORD had dawned upon certain dissident groups. It has been widely reported that these demonstrations were led by professional agitators. Several commentators claimed to have obtained evidence of communist infiltration among those who voted to strike in protest against the introduction of ORD. This is surprising because the attitude to sex in communist countries used to be far more rigid than it was in this country at that time.

60. It will be remembered that the same claims were made during the campaign to repeal the 1965 Abortion Act. The organizations supported by the Catholic church were especially active in pointing out that those who were demonstrating in favour of a liberal abortion law were the ignorant dupes of the Reds.[20] Some political commentators cited the collapse of democracy in Sweden last year as another example of the corrupting influence of communist-inspired sexual permissiveness.

61. We are not wholly convinced that sexual excess and Marxist

---

[20] They postulate that communist authorities may not be so tolerant of sexual freedom in their own countries, but the tactics in Britain are to encourage licentiousness while democratic government is in power in order to bring about its downfall in the general degradation that inevitably follows sexual permissiveness.

doctrines hang together. We believe that there may have been some people, not under communist influence, who genuinely saw the introduction of ORD as a threat to civil liberties. This was the view taken by the National Council for Civil Liberties. They insisted that the private acts of an individual inside his own home should not be the concern of the state unless it could be shown beyond reasonable doubt that these acts were harmful; it was manifest, they argued, that sexual acts were less harmful than they had been in the past.

62. The NCCL also led a vigorous campaign against the manner in which the legislation had been promulgated by Emergency Regulations. They maintained that Parliament was allowing its powers to be usurped by a few puritan members of the cabinet, who had made use of emergency powers which had been proclaimed for quite different reasons. A meeting was called in one of the committee rooms of the House of Commons so that the NCCL could put their views to members of Parliament, but only three were able to attend. The timing of the meeting was unfortunate because most members felt they should be in the chamber, where there was an important debate on the re-siting of the television cameras.

63. On the face of it there was some substance in the arguments put forward by the National Council for Civil Liberties, but it is a small organization with very little money and fewer than 5,000 members. We are forced to conclude that if the NCCL is unable to attract more funds and more members, then civil liberties are not an important issue for most people in this country and it is easy to understand why the government decided to ignore these puny protests.

64. In any case the strikes and demonstrations were to no avail. Recent history tells us that if the government can ride out the storm of protests for a few weeks, most campaigns will lose their impetus and the rule of law (or in this case, rule by regulation) can be restored. There were a few dogged protesters who refused to capitulate, notably at Notting Hill Gate where the occupants of a few youth collectives had to be forcibly fitted, and at Bournemouth where a detachment of the Royal Horse Guards had to be despatched to break up a para-military organization led by a posse of retired colonels who were protesting that the permitted number of orgasms was too high.

65. The original plan was to have everyone fitted by 1st January 1981. In the event the work was not completed until the middle of March by which time it could be said that the orgasms of everybody in the country were now safely under control.

## The Sexual Containment Act

66. Political commentators were taken by surprise when the Prime Minister introduced the Sexual Control (Orgasms) Bill in the new session. She said the clauses of the Bill were very similar to the Emergency Regulations of the previous year but she had been persuaded to introduce it now so as to counteract the accusation that the government was anxious to inhibit free discussion of this difficult subject. The Leader of the Opposition remarked that the Bill was rather pointless because the whole thing had been a *fait accompli* for more than eight months. The Prime Minister, however, pointed out that some people had been wearing ORD for only four months and it had not really been possible for the public to express their approval or disapproval until they had tried it out. She added that in any case the regulation would lapse in a few months when the State of Emergency became inoperative; the House had the option of passing a new law, or of prolonging the State of Emergency.

67. During the committee stage of the Bill, several MPs put down amendments which would make members of both Houses exempt from the provisions of the Act. They took as their precedent (albeit there were several they could have chosen) the Social Security Act, 1973 when it was arranged that self-employed members of Parliament should be exempt from paying the surcharge which was levied on their self-employed constituents.[21] The government, however, felt that this privilege should be granted only to Privy Councillors and a few other special cases.[22] When it became obvious that they were not going to be exempted themselves, members of Parliament did not press the amendment which would have granted exemption to certain categories of the physically handicapped, nor the amendment which would have exempted girls who

---

[21] See *Hansard* 24 January 1975
[22] The vexed question of exemptions has been a hive of controversy from the very start. It is discussed in more detail in Part III of this report.

had been raped. But they continued to go through the Bill clause by clause, concentrating on the technical details rather than the broader issues. At the report stage of the Bill, the colour of the male ORD was changed, a new procedure for seamen was laid down, the retiring age for Inspectors was raised from 65 to 70 and a number of other equally important amendments were proposed and accepted by the government.

68. In November the Sexual Containment Act, 1981 became law. The Royal Assent was delayed because the Queen was away for a few weeks on a much needed holiday after a strenuous season. There is no record of the Sovereign's comments at the moment when the Royal Assent was officially received. We have taken the liberty of making our own comment: Despite the misgivings and misunderstandings that arose when the idea of ORD was first mooted, the relative ease with which the population was fitted is a tribute to the morale and equanimity of the British people.

PART II

# SUMMARY OF INTERIM REPORTS

## Introduction

69. We have been granted access to the two confidential progress reports which were submitted to the Home Secretary, the Secretary of State for Scotland and the Secretary of State for Wales. As this is the first report that will be made public, we saw it as our duty to summarize these reports in so far as they explain why it was necessary to make certain alterations in the original plan after the Act had been in operation for one and two years respectively. We are aware that parts of these reports are still restricted for security reasons and this has required us to suppress some of the comments we might otherwise have made at this time.

70. It is not surprising that an innovation as far-reaching as this should have teething troubles. Some of them were not unexpected, but it is our view that other difficulties might have been anticipated when the original plan was being formulated. However, it is not within our terms of reference to proffer criticism or apportion blame. We have identified the six main problem areas encountered during the first two years in which the Act was in operation.

## Administrative Problems

71. During the first few months many people complained that the Referendaries were rude. All complaints were carefully investigated by the local Inspector and when the allegation involved an Inspector, the complaints procedure laid down under the Act provided for an Inspector from another region to carry out an investigation. The NCCL and others complained that this was not really an independent enquiry, but it was pointed out that only an Inspector could properly understand the problems of another. It was thought to be a situation similar to that which occurred when complaints were made against the police and the Act was drafted to

duplicate the same procedures when a senior police officer is called in to judge the actions of a policeman in a neighbouring force.

72. In the event it was usually found that there was little substance in these complaints. The Referendaries were rarely deemed to be guilty of serious rudeness, but sometimes they were insensitive or lacking in consideration when the subject was nervous or anxious. Some people are simply not used to undressing before a stranger.

73. The *Daily Express* campaigned for nuns to be exempt, but there are examples from the past which show that they have willingly submitted to more intimate examinations.[1] In our opinion this campaign was misguided. Women merely have to bare their breasts in order to have ORD fitted. It is the men who are required to undress completely so that ORD can be fitted under and round the genitals. There are reports that many men enjoy this, but there must be others who find it embarrassing.

74. Nevertheless it was recognized that there was some substance in a few of these complaints. When a Referendary has been checking and fitting over 40 ORDs a day, that is over 200 a week, there is a danger that he or she may become a little offhand. Case history no. 1 in Appendix B[2] is an example of how a Referendary may become insensitive to the feelings of a subject.

75. The solution was to improve recruitment and training. Many of the Inspectors were ex-servicemen and although beyond reproach as regards loyalty and discipline, some of them adopted a brusque manner and rugged language, which was mistaken for discourtesy. Most of the Referendaries had been traffic wardens, who had been made redundant when all private cars were banned in cities and towns. Although many of them carried out their duties satisfac-

---

[1] For example: Towne, J., 'Carcinoma of the Cervix in Nulliparous and Celibate Women', *American Journal of Obstetrics and Gynaecology,* 69: 606, 1955. Westwood, G., *Virgin Births in Convents,* Modern, 1980.

[2] Appendix B consists of a series of case histories obtained during the course of the survey which was commissioned for this report. Readers are warned that the language and descriptions used in this Appendix may give offence. The main body of the report is intended for the general public and for this reason we have avoided the use of obscene words with one exception; this is the case involving the late Archbishop of Canterbury where it was necessary to use a vulgar expression.

torily, it was found that some were lacking in sympathy and were rather inclined to ride roughshod over the feelings of the subject. A special effort was made to recruit Referendaries from other backgrounds and the government promised to employ more women as Inspectors.

76. The training programme was revised and extended so as to include special courses on public relations, counselling techniques and an elementary knowledge of behaviourist psychology. The Code of Practice has been revised and the ORD manual brought up to date. A large central training school is now established near Colchester in the buildings that were occupied by the University of Essex before it was closed down.

77. Despite these improvements it has been officially admitted that some unfortunate episodes have occurred. There have been a number of Referendaries who have accepted the lavish financial bribes offered by rich men and women intent on extending the range of their sex lives. Far more serious are the cases in which Referendaries have taken advantage of their privileged position and have accepted sexual favours. There is a period, which normally lasts only about ten minutes, when the ORD is being serviced and the subject is being interviewed before it is replaced or a new one fitted. It is during this period, when orgasms are not recorded, that the subject may be tempted to offer sexual inducements. Doubtless there have been occasions when these suggestions have been very explicit and the temptations have been considerable. It is to the credit of the corps that few Referendaries have offended against the Code. Nevertheless it was sensible to issue an order that whenever possible male subjects should be interviewed by men and female subjects by women.[3] Even this order did not entirely eliminate all the abuses because the authorities had not taken into account the power and extent of homosexual feelings.

78. When the original appointments were being made, it was suspected that an unexpectedly large proportion of the applicants were homosexually inclined. There did not seem at that time to be a very compelling reason for rejecting homosexual men or women who wished to become Referendaries. It was realized that some

---

[3] It was not possible to make this an invariable rule due to claims of sickness, holidays and other unavoidable staff absences.

would get a vicarious pleasure when fitting ORDs on to others of the same sex, but this did not seem to be a cause for alarm. It is well known that some of the best physiotherapists attached to football clubs get sexual pleasure from their activities and some exemplary nurses find it gratifying when they are required to shave the pubic hairs of patients of the same sex. The authorities did not anticipate any problem because all Referendaries had to wear ORDs and it was assumed that this would deter them from engaging in homosexual activities with subjects. However the details given in case history no. 2 in Appendix B indicate that the authorities may have underestimated the attractions of oral-genital activities.

79. There have been a few complaints about the National Computer. One woman received a card every Tuesday telling her to report to the Inspectorate. She dutifully went there and reported the mistake to the Referendary on five successive Tuesdays, but once a particular program is in the memory bank of this exceedingly intricate electronic brain, it is quite difficult to change its mind. After several unsuccessful attempts to alter the program, the engineers decided it would be less expensive to tell the woman to ignore the cards, which continue to arrive every Tuesday.

80. Complaints about alleged mistakes made by the National Computer are hardly ever resolved. For example, when the NC mistakenly decides that a boy is a girl, it is a very complex and time-consuming task to alter the program, and it is probably easier to change the sex of the boy.

## Legal Problems

81. ORD can only record the number of orgasms; it cannot prevent a subject from experiencing one. It follows from this that legislation on the compulsory wearing of ORD must be backed up by other sanctions. The penalties for exceeding the permitted number of orgasms (PNO) under the Sexual Containment Act, 1981, are as follows:

(1) Exceeding the PNO by less than five during a quarterly period is punishable on first conviction by a maximum fine of £50 and on subsequent convictions by a maximum fine of £250.

(2) Exceeding the PNO by more than five is punishable by an

unlimited fine or an order to attend a Hormone Adjustment Clinic as an out-patient.

(3) Persistently exceeding the PNO is punishable by an un-limited fine and detention in a Sexual Retraining Centre to undergo corrective therapy for a maximum of two years.

82. Inspectors are empowered to collect fines not exceeding £250 on the spot. No figure was put on the fines in clauses (2) or (3) so that the effects of inflation could be taken into account when award-ing a fine. No maximum period is specified for attendance at the Hormone Adjustment Clinic (HAC) because some subjects require more prolonged treatment than others. The medical director of the HAC is empowered to terminate the order which requires the subject to attend.

83. It was hoped that the sentence of detention at a Sexual Re-training Centre (SRC) for persistent offenders would act as a deter-rent, but this hope has not been fulfilled and we are concerned that so many people have been sent to these institutions. It may be that the judges over-reacted when they were given the chance to sentence subjects to a place which, unlike the ordinary prison, promised to reform as well as incarcerate. In reality the term 'corrective therapy' may be over-sanguine for it has been found that a regrettably large proportion of those offenders relapse even after a long period at the SRC. Nevertheless, we are not persuaded that the time has come to introduce more severe penalties because every attempt should be made to get the persistent offender to understand that the object is, not to hinder him, but to help him control his wayward sexual drive.

84. We have received representations from the Carnival of White and other groups, who have suggested there should be a stronger element of public disgrace in the penalties. We appreciate the force of this argument but the effects are not wholly predictable. At one time the *Sun* newspaper sought permission to print the full names of all the people who had exceeded the PNO by more than 15 in each quarterly period. At first the Home Office was inclined to favour this idea and considered the possibility of relaxing the censorship on all press reports about ORD. But further enquiries revealed that it was intended to publish the top twenty names in the form of a league table and negotiations had been started with London Plastic

Industries[4] to sponsor a competition with special badges and coloured hats for those who had experienced the highest number of orgasms during the previous quarter. These plans did not meet with the approval of the Home Secretary who feels that the public have an ambivalent attitude to sex and too much publicity of any kind may be double-edged.

85. There have been a number of test cases brought by aggrieved subjects in the last two years, but none of them have succeeded in challenging the legality of the procedures of the Act itself. The most usual case is that in which the subject claims that the ORD he has been wearing has given an incorrect reading due to a fault in the mechanism. It is always difficult to deal with subjects who maintain that their ORD must be wrong because it is not possible to give positive proof that the reading is correct. All that can be done is to assure the subject that faults in the mechanism are rare. In some ways it is similar to the circumstances when someone complains that their telephone bill is wrong; as neither the Post Office nor the subscriber can produce convincing proof that the meter reading is right or wrong, the only possible solution is to accept the word of the official. Once this has been explained to the subject, only the really contentious will continue to press the case.

86. We are informed that the Inspectors are not intractable and are often prepared to give the subject the benefit of the doubt in reasonable cases. For example there was one subject whose ORD registered 79 orgasms at the end of the 13 week period, although she maintained that she had experienced fewer than 20 orgasms as her husband had been away for part of the period. After some discussion it was agreed that there were signs of wear, which might have caused the second digit of the recording mechanism to have slipped. After further discussions the Inspector compromised and decided to charge her for only 29 orgasms. This meant she had to pay a small fine but at least she was spared the embarrassment of having to attend the HAC as an outpatient.

87. One subject decided to take his case to the European Commission of Human Rights at Strasbourg. The government was anxious to avoid this because Britain had already received more

---

[4] A manufacturer of condoms.

adverse decisions from this court than any other country in Europe. However, the subject was not prepared to consider any of the compromises offered by Home Office officials in a series of acrimonious meetings with his lawyers. Consequently the government felt it had been placed in an invidious position and announced even before the case had started that it did not intend to comply with the decision of the Commission. It is our view that this was a tactical mistake. It would have been more felicitous to have opposed the case in court on the grounds that this was not within the framework of the Human Rights Convention and so beyond the jurisdiction of the Commission. However, we are of the opinion that neither the government's ill-advised action nor the decision of the Commission of Human Rights will have much practical effect on the public's attitude to ORD.

88. When ORD was first introduced under the emergency regulations, the appeal for voluntary restraint went largely unheeded. It is often said that the British always respond more readily to calls for voluntary action than they do to compulsory edicts. We wish this were true, but events have shown that the appeals for voluntary sexual restraint were no more successful than the appeals for wage restraints in 1974–5. We conclude, therefore, that the penalties introduced under the Sexual Containment Act are necessary.

89. Another familiar saying is that you cannot make people moral by passing laws,[5] but this Act has made people count every sexual act, even though it has not succeeded in making each sexual act count.

## Technical Problems

90. In the previous section we noted that there have been a number of cases when the subject has complained that the mechanism broke down and gave a faulty reading. All of these cases have been investigated by Inspectors under the complaints procedure laid down in the ORD Code of Practice. In almost every instance the Inspectors have reported that the complaint has been caused by

---

[5] For example: 'We all know that you cannot (regretfully) make people good by Act of Parliament . . .' Robinson, John, *The Place of Law in the Field of Sex*, Sexual Law Reform Society, 1973.

C

subject-error; sometimes it is due to simple miscounting or forget-fulness, and at other times it is due to a misunderstanding of the nature of an orgasm.

91. For example, some subjects think that an orgasm experienced through fantasy would not register on ORD. From the earliest days of sexual research, investigators[6] have reported the ability of men and women to reach orgasm without touching the genitals. It is thought that this is the origin of the expression, 'Look, no hands!' Orgasms resulting from fantasies produce the same basic physio-logical response in the body and are therefore recorded on ORD just like any other orgasm.

92. Both the confidential progress reports have stressed that no evidence of serious mechanical failure has been found. On the contrary, the broad indications are that ORD is an efficient piece of electronic engineering. Consequently the only major technical change since the introduction of ORD has been the development of Mark II.

93. It had been anticipated that there would be a certain amount of vandalism and damage done to ORD as a result either of mind-less frustration or a more premeditated attempt to make it tem-porarily inoperative. Lovers have been known to boast to each other about the feats of prolonged ecstasy they would accomplish if only ORD could be switched off for a few hours. But this problem of vandalism had been foreseen during the trial periods. Obviously it would be much too painful for a subject to try to remove ORD altogether, but a mechanism as delicate as this cannot be made absolutely impregnable. So both the male and female versions were designed in such a way that the appliance was sealed after each fitting so that, if anyone attempted to tamper with ORD, this would be immediately apparent to the Referendary at the next visit to the Inspectorate.

94. Anyone who was found to have a broken seal was fined £50

[6] Bloch, Ivan, *The Sexual Life of our Time and its Relation to Modern Civilization*, Rebman, 1908.
Kisch, E. H., *The Sexual Life of Women in its Psychological, Pathological and Hygienic Aspects*, Allied Books, 1926.
Klumbies, G. and Kleinsorge, H., 'Circulatory dangers and prophylaxis during orgasm', *Int. J. Sexol.*, 4: 61–66, 1950.

and it was assumed that this would be a sufficient deterrent. Unfortunately the sequel to this kind of vandalism was not fully appreciated at the time. Attempts to make ORD inoperative were often unsuccessful and even the most ingenious manipulation by a skilled electronic engineer did not always stop ORD from continuing to record every orgasm. But what officials had failed to take into account was the attitude of mind of the vandals once the seal was broken. The offenders realized they would be in trouble when they had to report to the Inspectorate and as long as they were under the impression (often mistaken) that ORD was no longer recording, they did not restrain themselves. Even if the subjects realized that they had not managed to stop ORD, once the seal was broken they knew they would be fined and constraint was lacking. 'Might as well be hanged for a ram as a lamb,' as one man remarked when he reported to the Referendary with a broken seal and 17 orgasms over the PNO.

95. The problem was the period between the time when the seal was broken and the next visit to the Inspectorate. If the damage was done soon after the first fitting, it could be as much as twelve weeks before the subject received the next card from the National Computer summoning him to the Inspectorate. There were several cases of men who broke the seal and then heedlessly indulged in numerous orgasms for the remaining weeks.

96. It is even more serious when a woman's seal is broken. We have been told about several unfortunate episodes; eg, a woman who has been law abiding for months or years quite suddenly breaks out and throws all caution to the wind. It is almost as if women need legal restraints more than men. Perhaps this is because the female is capable of having orgasms in rapid succession and over a longer period than is the case with the male. Some women were quite unrestrained in the number of orgasms they had as long as they believed that ORD was not recording. In Appendix B there is the evidence of a young woman (case history no. 3) who had over 40 orgasms in the ten days after breaking the seal before she was apprehended by a Referendary. The mind boggles at the number of orgasms she might have experienced in the 10 weeks before she was due to visit the Inspectorate again.

97. The solution was a most ingenious invention, originally the

brain-child of a private individual[7] who had made a life-long study of methods by which other people's sexual activities could be restricted. His idea was improved and remodelled by workers at the government research institutes and is now known as ORD (Mark II). If the seal of this device is broken, it will activate a klaxon which has been cleverly incorporated into both the male and female version of ORD without noticeably increasing the size. The klaxon continues to sound until the subject visits the Inspectorate. The key that will switch it off is only issued to Inspectors.

98. This is a most effective deterrent and at the same time brings in that element of public participation that so many people have requested. A subject hurrying to the Inspectorate with an activated klaxon is bound to be the object of considerable public attention, especially if he has to walk down a crowded street or travel by bus.

99. Although government engineers were reasonably confident about the mechanical effectiveness of ORD (Mark II), there were some doubts about the sociological aspects. Accordingly it was decided to stage a pilot run in one town and the authorities chose Bradford because of its poor record over the first year. When each subject came in for servicing, the Referendary fitted the Mark II ORD and explained about the klaxon.

100. It was intended to keep the pilot secret and a G Notice[8] was issued to the media. But the news spread quickly and soon became common knowledge in West Yorkshire, partly because the inhabitants of Bradford were proud because their town had been chosen; it kindled the ancient rivalry with Leeds who 'were only known for their football team, but we are well known for our sex buzzers.'

101. Unfortunately some wild rumours soon spread throughout the North. One rumour was to the effect that ORD (Mark II) was attached to the back of the neck and the klaxon was activated whenever the subject's brain received any sort of sexual stimulation, but we are reliably informed by government researchers that such

---

[7] Although his name has never been made public officially, it is well known that he is a prolific author, literary critic and letter-writer who lives in East Anglia.
[8] Unlike the earlier arrangement, G Notices are compulsory with specified penalties for journalists and broadcasters who publish items banned in the interests of national security.

a device is not yet a practical proposition. Nevertheless these stories aroused public curiosity and crowds travelled from Leeds, Harrogate, Huddersfield and elsewhere for a day out, hoping to 'hear the horns', as they put it. Most of them were disappointed, of course, because even in Bradford the number of people tampering with their ORDs on any one day must be quite small.

102. After only a few weeks the Bradford pilot run convinced the government that they could expect to receive public co-operation and the order was given to fit Mark II ORDs to the rest of the population. Most people now recognize the sound made by the klaxon and some of them feel impelled to take action when they hear it. There have been a few unfortunate incidents when a crowd has over-reacted and the subject with the klaxon sounding has required police protection so that he could get to the Inspectorate. The police have a difficult task in these cases. Clearly it is their duty to save all subjects from being seriously injured. But the police are also the servants of the public, in our view at least, and in the present climate of opinion, a subject with an activated klaxon must expect to be abused and even molested by members of the public.

103. The most distressing episode which has been reported to us occurred last year when a group of young people under the influence, it is alleged, of XBP[9] staged a demonstration in Trafalgar Square of what they called 'mutual ORD smashing'. The police were rather slow to comprehend the real significance of this demonstration; they thought the young people were about to bathe in the fountains; or possibly stage a new outbreak of old fashioned 'streaking'.[10] But as more and more seals were broken, more and

---

[9] XBP is one of the new recreational drugs which induces contentment if taken in the specified doses, but which leads to irresponsible geniality if the stated dose is exceeded. It is not known how these young people obtained the drug because XBP may only be prescribed by doctors to subjects over 45 who hold important executive positions.

[10] 'Streaking' was a strange outbreak of irrational behaviour during 1972–3 when men took off their clothes and ran through a crowded area. No one produced a satisfactory explanation for this phenomenon at the time, but it is now thought that the tight fitting trousers fashionable at that period may have caused unbearable constriction. The appearance of those who were 'streaking' was so unsightly that it is safe to conclude that it had very little to do with sexual stimulation.

more klaxons sounded off and it is said that at the height of the demonstration the noise could be heard in the Houses of Parliament. The police were in a difficult position because it is not an arrestable offence to be sounding the klaxon, but after a few minutes hesitation, they sent for reinforcements and arrested 14 men and 32 women for insulting behaviour likely to cause a breach of the peace. There were some ugly scenes at Bow Street as some of the young people had to be held down so that an Inspector could switch off the klaxons. At the trial the judge said he thought it was more high spirits than sexual debauchery, but he could not overlook the damage to public property and sentenced them all to three months imprisonment.

104. There have been surprisingly few objections to ORD (Mark II). The most serious complaint is that sometimes the klaxon sounds even though the seal has not been broken. The evidence we have received from Inspectors rejects this complaint; they maintain that there are hairline cracks on the seal in nearly all cases when the subjects have complained about their klaxons being faulty; and they express the opinion that these cracks in the seal must be caused by tampering with the ORD, or at any rate fingering it, or playing the fool in some other way. However, there is the well known case of the film actress whose klaxon started to sound when she was before the TV cameras being interviewed by a Mr M. Parkinson, and we have received reports of several other cases when the klaxon has sounded for no known reason. We feel bound to accept that there are cases (probably not more than 5 per cent) where the mechanism has been faulty and the klaxon has sounded prematurely.[11] We also concede that this could lead to considerable embarrassment, especially as Inspectors on night duty work on a rota system and the unfortunate subject may have to travel ten miles or more before it can be switched off. We would further like to suggest that those who suffer in this way should be entitled to compensation, but we are in some difficulty here because the conflicting evidence makes adjudication well nigh impossible.

105. It has been in our minds to recommend that an independent tribunal be set up to hear all complaints, but when this was

---

[11] One example of this is reported in case history no. 4 in Appendix B.

suggested in an earlier report, the Union of Inspectors and Refer-endaries threatened to call a strike. We can do no more than defer to the privately held (albeit never openly expressed) view of most magistrates that so long as no more than 10 per cent of the innocent are found guilty, justice is being done.

106. The other objections to ORD (Mark II) are more trivial. There have been complaints that when subjects rush into the In-spectorate with the klaxon sounding, it upsets the appointment system and Inspectors should refuse to attend to them unless the waiting-room is empty. But Inspectors maintain that it is not safe to leave a person with an activated klaxon in a small room with other people who are likely to be vindictive. We would rather leave this to the good sense of the Inspectors and do not intend to make any specific recommendation. Nor do we intend to take any action on the objection from the RSPCA who complain that the klaxon is too loud and is the cause of distress to dogs and other pets. One grievance we do take rather more seriously is the allegation that the police often use their cars to take privileged persons (including their own colleagues in the Force) to the Inspectorate with the siren on the police car blaring out so as to drown the sound from the ORD's klaxon.

107. Our conclusion is that the introduction of ORD (Mark II) has achieved all that it was intended to do. Naturally we are con-cerned that some innocent people are being caused considerable em-barrassment, but the government has arranged for Inspectorates to be open during the night and on public holidays to deal with these emergencies. No other modifications are required and we are able to report that from a technical point of view this device is an efficient piece of electronic engineering.

108. Unfortunately the sound of the klaxon seems to bring out in some people a censorious indignation not far removed from envy.[12] These feelings of resentment are very powerful. The in-troduction of the Mark II version of ORD has successfully checked vandalism, but it seems to have brought to the surface deep psycho-social emotions which we think are rather disturbing.

---

[12] Case history no. 5 provides several examples of the pitiless opprobrium heaped on a subject who has activated his klaxon.

**Pathological Problems**

109. As we stated in Part I, ORD records every orgasm whatever may be the mode of stimulation. Consequently masturbation by a male or female subject is always recorded and most people agree that it should be counted in the PNO. If this were not so, there would be an undesirable increase in the frequency of masturbation. Some writers have suggested that this would be a contribution towards the problem of overpopulation because habitual masturbation would leave people too tired to have sexual intercourse. But this argument is unconvincing because the Sexual Containment Act has already had the effect of reducing the frequency of sexual intercourse without increasing the amount of masturbation. Furthermore we feel that people should be discouraged from preferring the inward-looking pleasures of masturbation to the more companionable rewards of sexual intercourse. Indeed the tendency to prefer masturbation to sexual intercourse is an insidious temptation because it is now known that the intensity of orgasm is greater during masturbation than at any other time.[13]

110. But the problem of nocturnal emissions ('wet dreams' as they are called colloquially) is much more controversial and there are many who feel that they should not be counted in the PNO. It is argued that these nocturnal emissions are quite involuntary and a frequent occurrence among young men; furthermore religious and moral youths are more likely to have involuntary emissions of semen during the night precisely because they are refraining from premarital sexual intercourse. There are also some unfortunate cases where married men have no orgasms to spare for their wives because they cannot help using up their PNO while asleep.

111. But nocturnal emissions are often the result of erotic dreams and the line between them and masturbation is difficult to draw. Some men can experience an orgasm through exercising their imagination without so much as touching the genitals.[14] In any case

---

[13] 'Understandably (sic) the maximum physiologic intensity of orgasmic response subjectively reported or objectively recorded has been achieved by self-regulated mechanical or automanipulative techniques.' Masters, W. and Johnson, V., *Human Sexual Response*, Little Brown, 1966.
[14] Rohleder, H., *Die Masturbation: Eine Monographic für Ärtze, Pädagogen und gebildete Eltern*, (4th ed.), Fischers medizinische Buchhandlung, 1921. See also the references in the footnote to paragraph 91.

the physiology of the orgasm is the same no matter how it is achieved, whether it is nocturnal emissions, masturbation or sexual intercourse,[15] and it is quite impossible for ORD to distinguish between them.

112. Various devices have been tried in the past to stop nocturnal emissions, notably the clip of steel, a contraption with metal spikes which discouraged involuntary (and voluntary) erections.[16] Our attitudes today are more humane. Indeed we have been informed that the authorities are anxious to help those who are troubled by nocturnal emissions and other spontaneous orgasms; Home Office officials are not lacking in human compassion, even though this may sometimes appear to be the case. Inspectors arrange for subjects who suffer from this complaint to attend a Hormone Adjustment Clinic (HAC), but they have been given clear instructions that this must not be regarded as a punishment.

113. At the HAC the subject will be given an oestrogen compound which will diminish his sexual appetite. Many experimenters[17] have found that the sex drive can be altered by varying the blood levels of hormones. Oestrogen or synthetic oestrogen products are used to reduce the male's sexual desire. Once the correct dose has been calculated, the subject is allowed to take the oestrogen prepared in tablet form, so that he can take a supply home with him. This is because he is not treated as a criminal. He is sick.

114. Administrators at the HACs do not refer to these subjects as being over-sexed. They are said to be suffering from 'sex-steroid starvation' and are put on a course of 'endocrine replacement therapy'. This is in contrast to the offenders who are directed by the court to attend the HACs where they are given oestrogen compounds in order to curb their sex drive. Offenders cannot be trusted to administer their own doses of oestrogen and have to be treated with 'strap-on' drugs. This is a small phial which is placed under

---

[15] Calderone, M. S., *Release from Sexual Tensions*, Random House, 1960. Rasmussen, J. and Albrechtsen, O. K., 'Fibrinolytic Activity in Human Seminal Plasma', *Fertil, Steril.* 11: 264–277, 1960
[16] Blackburn, Thomas, *A Clip of Steel*, MacGibbon and Kee, 1969.
[17] Foote, R. M., 'Diethylstilboestrol in the management of psychopathic states', *Journal of Nervous and Mental Disease*, 99, 923–935, 1944. Greenblatt, R. B., 'Hormonal factors in libido', *Journal of Clinical Endocrinology*, 3, 305–306, 1943.

the patient's skin by means of a special instrument called an 'introducer'. This allows a certain amount of the drug to filter through direct into the blood stream. When a voluntary patient swallows a tablet the oestrogen has to go through the stomach and liver, and it loses some of its strength; some patients need three pills a day to keep their sexual desires quiescent. But when a phial is strapped on to an offender, the drug is slowly filtering through his body all the time and can last for as long as six months. The main advantage of this addition to the therapeutic armamentarium is that it does not require the compliance of the patient.

115. Many articles have been written on the subject of the hormonal control of sexual behaviour (see, for example, Young and Gay)[18] and it would be superfluous to discuss the technical aspects in this report. Although experiments with cocks,[19] chimpanzees and human beings have been going on for many years, it is only recently that it has been possible to measure hormone levels in blood serum with any accuracy. Even now it takes a little time to get the balance right because the medication is rather slow acting and so offenders have to be treated as in-patients for the first few weeks.

116. Men usually produce small amounts of female hormone (just as women produce small amounts of male hormone). The problem is to get the correct balance. A certain amount of oestrogen will reduce the sex drive in man (although it will not affect his sexual orientation).[20] But if he is given too much, there are un-

---

[18] Young, W., Gay, R. and Phoenix, C., 'Hormones and Sexual Behaviour', Science, 143, 212–218, 1964.

[19] In cocks the effects are quite dramatic. 'Hen communities produce a social hierachy or pecking order, with the cock bossing all, and the most powerful and aggressive of the hens pecking at all her sisters below.' Feeding oestrogen to a cock reduces his social status; he allows hens to peck him, assumes female postures and attempts to mate with other cocks. 'Of course the analogy between this behaviour and human homosexuality must not be pressed too far.' From West, Donald, Homosexuality, Duckworth, 1967.

[20] Oestrogens will not turn a male homosexual into a heterosexual. Homosexual men have often been given large doses of oestrogen (e.g. Glass, S. J., et al., 'Sex hormone studies in male homosexuality', Journal of Clinical Endocrinology, 26, 590–594, 1940). It tended to reduce their homosexual activities, but it also destroyed all heterosexual interests. These cases were described as successful cures, because the doctors felt it was better to be sexless than homosexual.

pleasant side effects such as the stimulation of feminine breast development, which is painful and may be embarrassing when swimming and on other sporting occasions. If a man's breasts become too large, he can return to the HAC and have them amputated. A number of surgeons have made a speciality of this work and the breasts can be detruncated quite neatly.

117. It is unfortunate that economic reasons make it necessary for offenders and sick (voluntary) subjects to attend for treatment at the same place. Most HACs are located in the old VD clinics, which are not so busy now. Although many of them are rather dingy and uninviting, there is the advantage that these old clinics usually have their own waiting rooms apart from the main hospital buildings. There has been more than one unfortunate mistake when the main waiting room in the hospital has been used and an attendant has confused two people with similar names. We feel that people who are ill and attending as out-patients should not be subjected to the additional inconvenience of having their sex drive artificially curbed by mistake.

118. We think it is right that subjects who have spontaneous orgasms should be treated as voluntary patients with an unbalanced endocrine system. This is all part of the progressive tendency to regard non-conformity as a sickness.[21] Nevertheless we must face the fact that men who have too many nocturnal emissions must attend the HAC regularly, or else a measure of compulsion becomes inevitable.

119. Very few cases of involuntary orgasms in women have been reported although such cases have been noted in popular and scientific literature.[22] Women who have attended HACs have been treated with hormone preparations with varying degrees of success. Some of them produce unfortunate side effects like falling hair, a coarsening of the features and a beard on the chin; voluntary patients should not be asked to tolerate this, even though some doctors feel ethically justified in requiring female offenders to put

---

[21] For example, we no longer treat people who smoke cannabis as if they are criminals, but as sick people who need our help.
[22] For example: Dickinson, R. L. and Beam, L., *The Single Woman*, Williams and Wilkins, 1934. Stekel, W., *Frigidity in Woman in Relation to Her Love Life*, Liveright, 1926. Westwood, G., *How to be Single and Sexy*, Modern, 1979.

up with these side effects. Until recently women who came to HACs were treated with tranquillizers; unfortunately some subjects who have been treated with these drugs became addicted to them and have required up to 60 tranquillizers a day. Most HACs now use other pharmaceutical compounds to help women to be systematically cleansed of their offending sexual drive.

120. If a man takes oestrogen in large quantities over a long period, his testicular tissues will atrophy. In other words, it will have the same effect as castration. Indeed some people maintain that castration is a better solution.[23] They argue that oestrogen treatment is not always successful in diminishing sexual feelings and one has to keep on giving it to the subject which makes the treatment expensive; it is better and cheaper to castrate. The feasibility of this contention is discussed in Part III (paragraphs 185–190).

121. Hormone treatment has some unfortunate disadvantages. It is not strictly a cure because sexual desire returns if the subject stops taking the tablets. Hormone injections interfere with the little understood endocrine balance within the human body. There are reports of synthetic steroids causing jaundice, diabetes and thrombosis.[24] Some doctors think that oestrogen stops bones developing and say that it should not be given to adolescents – just the people who have the most difficulty controlling their nocturnal emissions.[25] The most serious doubts about the possible side effects of hormone treatment are the risks of breast cancer in men as well as women. One study[26] compared 94 patients with cancer with a control group and the analysis revealed that hormone treatment had been given to 57 per cent of the patients and only 15 per cent of the controls. It is fair to say that the administrators of the HACs are not being complacent about the existence of this link between hormone treatment and cancer. Already a new research has been started in which

---

23 For example: Hackfield, A. W., 'Uber die Kastration bei vierzig sexuell Abnormen', *Monatschrift fur Psychiatrie und Neurologie*, 87, 1, 1933.
24 Cooper, Alan, 'A pilot study of mesterolone in impotence', *Psychopharmacologia*, 26, 379–386, 1972. Beaumont, George, 'Sexual side-effects of drugs', *British Journal of Sexual Medicine*, 1: 5, 10–12, 1974.
25 On the other hand oestrogen is said to be beneficial for old men who have cancer of the prostate.
26 Zeil, H., and Finkle, W., in the *New England Journal of Medicine*, 293, 1167, 1975.

half the offenders of one HAC are to be given a medical inspection every year, while the other half will be used as a control group and so will not be checked. After a few years it will be possible to see if the control group develop more tumours than the screened group. There are, of course, good precedents for doctors allowing patients to be untreated so that they can follow the development of a disease. In the course of the Tuskegee Study which began 40 years ago in the US state of Alabama, 200 black males suffering from syphilis were denied proper medical treatment for the disease so that eventual examinations of their corpses could establish what damage it does to the human body. Seventy four of the untreated syphilitics were still alive when the results of the Tuskegee Study were made public.[27]

122. There has been an unfortunate increase in the number of cases of rape since the introduction of ORD. Girls who go to the police after being raped do not always get treated very well. There is still this feeling that a girl could have prevented it if she had really tried, but this attitude is no longer justified (and probably never was) now that Parliament has refused to make an exception in rape cases. It is hard to believe that any girl would allow one of her permitted number of orgasms to be taken away from her by force without putting up a fight.

123. Criminologists[28] have produced evidence that a rapist usually attacks a woman towards the end of his quarterly period when he still has some PNOs left over. There are signs that the sexually unsuccessful tend to look upon the PNO as a kind of ration and they feel they are legally entitled to have sexual intercourse 27 times a quarter. These sexually deprived men may have some difficulty in finding willing partners.

124. Commercial prostitution has decreased since ORD was

[27] The American Medical Association issued a statement condemning this experiment because these men did not *volunteer* to have treatment withheld. But it is really expecting too much of patients, even if they are offenders, to make this kind of sacrifice voluntarily; all one can do is to make sure that their relatives are aware that their suffering is not in vain because future generations will benefit from the knowledge obtained by allowing the disease to take its natural course.

[28] *Five Thousand Cases of Incest, Rape, Sadism, Necrophilia and Coprophagia,* collected and studied by the Cambridge University Institute of Criminology, CUP, 1981.

introduced and it has become almost impossible for a call-girl to make a decent living. Men have become more fastidious about where, how and with whom they have an orgasm. But a few dissatisfied rejects remain and there may be a case for establishing prostitution as a social service for the sexually handicapped.[29]

125. Lack of sexual success is, of course, just as common among women as it is among men and any arrangement for the supply of surrogate partners will have to be made for both sexes. We have been told about some cases in which women force men to have orgasms against their will. Some of these episodes are almost equivalent to rape; case history no. 6 in Appendix B is but one example of where a group of women have sexually assaulted a man.

126. It has been put to us that there are a large number of women, not all of them ill-favoured, with pressing sexual needs. It is beyond our competence to say whether this is true or not. But if there really is this urgent demand, it should not be too difficult to recruit a corps of capable male prostitutes.

127. It has been widely reported[30] that some women have regular sexual intercourse but never experience an orgasm. This is generally thought of as a disability and many pages in many sex manuals give advice to women on how to obtain an orgasm. At first sight one might have supposed that the Categorical Society and other guardians of moral standards would approve of women who were sexually not too responsive, but in fact they are censured. If a woman does not have an orgasm, her sexual acts will not be recorded by ORD and this, in the view of the moral guardians, is a form of cheating and a way round the Sexual Containment Act. However, no pro-

---

[29] 'Recruits to the ranks of the oldest profession would be of an entirely different character if a more positive attitude were taken towards prostitution. If we thought of them as medical auxiliaries, instead of whores and harlots, it is probable that the calibre of the recruits would improve and young people of both sexes would not be ashamed to enter the ranks of a worthwhile profession. They would be trained in social welfare and part of their job would be to attend to the non-sexual needs of their clients. Courtesy, conversation and a good knowledge of inceptive techniques would become important aspects of the work.' Schofield, Michael, *Promiscuity*, Gollancz, 1976.

[30] Brown, D., *Female orgasm and sexual inadequacy (a survey of the literature)*. Presented at a Conference of American Association of Marriage Counsellors, Chicago, 1964.

posal apart from castigation has been put forward and no edifying solution springs to mind. It would, of course, be possible to administer androgen compounds in order to make them more sexually responsive but this is not really in line with existing government policy.

128. An attempt to find a hormonal solution to this problem is unlikely to be successful because failure to achieve an orgasm during sexual intercourse is more likely to be due to psychosocial factors. In any case we do not think these women need be a cause for serious concern. It is a characteristic of ORD, and this is why the concept is so adroit, that it is a two-way regulator. A woman may have sexual intercourse without that event being recorded on ORD, but it is likely that her partner will have an orgasm which would, of course, be recorded on his ORD. So the restrictive effect is still present. Even if the woman is promiscuous, she has still got to find men who are willing to spare an orgasm for her. It can be appreciated, therefore, that ORD is a resourceful contrivance for controlling the sexual drive.

## Diplomatic Problems

129. From the earliest days it was realized that it would be impossible to make exceptions for tourists and visitors. Inspectorates were established at all ports and airfields so that everyone entering the country could be fitted and the regulations explained to them. As few of the Referendaries could speak any foreign language, a certain amount of confusion was inevitable at first, but now leaflets in all the main languages are available at these Inspectorates. Even so we feel that our embassies and consulates abroad might do more to warn intending visitors about the Sexual Containment Act and how it would affect them. There have been cases when old ladies have been taken by surprise at the Inspectorate because they were under the impression that they were being searched for contraband by customs officials. It has been put to us by the Minister of Tourism and others that the prospect of being fitted with ORD has been an inducement for some visitors and has given an extra fillip to the tourist trade, but this must be due to a misunderstanding of the real purpose of the device.

130. A similar misunderstanding must be the explanation for

the remark of the East African dictator who, when told that he would have to wear ORD during his visit to England, replied: 'I doubt if they'll have one big enough to fit me.' A special Inspectorate has been attached to the VIP suite at Heathrow and we have not been informed of any international incident or diplomatic protest from visiting dignatories.

131. The advent of large jets has meant that passengers arrive at airfields in waves of 500 people or more. This puts a considerable strain on the Referendaries and long queues have formed outside the Inspectorate. However, passengers usually get through Immigration and Inspectorate formalities long before the baggage handlers have managed to get the luggage off the plane and on to the airport carousel.

132. British tourists are now required to wear ORD if they are going to be out of the country for less than four weeks. Originally British holidaymakers were allowed to have it removed, but a year's experience of the Sexual Containment Act revealed that too many people were going abroad for short periods in order to indulge in sexual activities. The sexual behaviour of foreigners is not, of course, the concern of the British government, but the authorities were worried about the number of subjects taking British girls, not necessarily their wives, on day trips to France and week-end charter flights to Majorca. The Chancellor of the Exchequer felt that it was necessary to seek these new powers, not so much for moral reasons, but to save foreign exchange. We appreciate the force of his argument, but we wonder if the hurt pride of the local inhabitants in foreign resorts at cross purposes with the equivocal holidaymakers really makes it a worthwhile economy, particularly as it is necessary sometimes to fly out a Referendary to turn off an activated klaxon.

133. The government of the Republic of Ireland paid a compliment to the success of ORD when it sent diplomatic representatives to ask if the country could be associated with the scheme. The Irish government agreed to pay half the cost of the ORDs if the British would set up and man a network of Inspectorates throughout United Ireland. Although this would be an extra cost to the British taxpayer, the Irish government maintained that this would hardly be more expensive than the existing situation. At present

a very large number of Irish volunteers come over to England to get fitted up free on the NHS and then return without surrendering their ORDs. According to these Irishmen, this is merely continuing the tradition that the Irish have special privileges (or 'rights' as they call them) denied to other aliens.

134. It is estimated that about 30 per cent of all Irish males are now voluntarily wearing ORDs. The Irish women do not seem to be so interested in the device. No government Inspectorates have been set up, but there are some that are run privately, charging a modest fee to have the ORD read, and a larger fee to switch off an activated klaxon – a rare event in Ireland. These privately-run inspectorates are staffed by men from the English corps who are being tempted to work in these Irish centres; the pay for Referendaries is not so high as in England, but the work is more inviting because they are not compelled to wear ORDs themselves, not even during working hours. Irishmen who visit the private inspectorates do not make themselves liable for a fine if they exceed the PNO, but they like to have the information so that they can tell the priest at confession.

135. We do not see why the Irish should expect us to provide them with ORDs. Statistics are notoriously hard to obtain, but our understanding is that the Irish male is rather less orgasmic than most. If it is true, as we suspect, that the typical Irishman does not like sex, we deem this to be his problem, not ours.

## Religious and Moral Problems

136. The Christian church has always maintained a negative attitude to sex[31] and the government had hoped that the Sexual Containment Act would get the approval of religious leaders. It was supposed that any reduction in the overall amount of sex would receive support from the church, but when ORD was first introduced, it got no more than grudging approval.

137. It may be that 27 orgasms every thirteen weeks is still too much by the standards of St Paul.[32] Certainly there were some

---

[31] With the notable exception of the late Archbishop of Canterbury.
[32] 'I say therefore to the unmarried and widows, It is good for them if they abide even as I. But if they cannot contain, let them marry: for it is better to marry than to burn.' I *Corinthians* VII, 8–9.

D

clergymen who said the PNO was too indulgent and a sop to lascivious living. Surprisingly there were other churchmen who said that the PNO was too small, that it would portend the decline of the Christian population, and that it would cause unemployment among teachers in church schools. Both sides were able to find relevant passages in the Bible to support their views.[33]

138. Although the clergy tended to argue about details, we believe there is another explanation for their lack of enthusiasm at the start. The churches, whether established or not, are reluctant to give their approval to any innovation. It usually takes a little time before religious leaders can be sure that they know God's Will on modern matters; understandably the religious authorities need a period of prayer and contemplation before they can be certain that they have correctly heard the Word of God on something as neoteric as ORD.

139. At the time of writing, it is the Roman Catholic Church that seems to be most favourably disposed to ORD and this has raised the hopes of the government salesmen in their attempts to export the female model to some of the South American countries. Confidence has also been increased by two sentences in a recent Papal Encyclical, which some interpreters say might be a reference to the Sexual Containment Act. There are others, however, who wonder if the Holy Father really had ORD in mind when he spoke these words.

'It is one of the finest and most noble aspirations of man to search for ever new ways of ensuring the control of sexual extravagance. The Church, illuminated and enriched by Divine Revelation, reaffirms her position and unequivocally proclaims that it is contrary to natural law to interfere with the procreative and uniting function of the conjugal relationship but exculpation is available for teachers and monitors. (38, Pius XIII, 1983).[34]

140. The government attaches great importance to obtaining religious approval. Although it is clear that most people now accept

---

[33] 'To be carnally minded is death.' *Romans* VIII, 6. 'Be fruitful, and multiply, and replenish the earth.' *Genesis* I, 28.
[34] When the Cardinal Archbishop of Westminster was asked if these words were a reference to the Sexual Containment Act, he replied: 'Consult approved texts and act prudently.'

ORD with or without the blessing of the church, support from the religious authorities will enhance the solemnity of each occasion. Already there are signs that some people take a flippant attitude to ORD. For example, there is the new fashion of wearing ORDs on both breasts; unlicensed manufacturers have brought out dummy models, some of which are quite good imitations of the real thing. The police report the outbreak of a nasty game, somewhat after the fashion of Russian roulette; a gang of boys hold a girl captive and cut one of the leads from the reactor[35] to her ORD. If it is the dummy, no harm is done, but if it is the real ORD, the klaxon will sound. The name of the game, we are told, is 'Tit Soundings'.

141. We have it on good authority that there are no plans to place legal restrictions on these imitations of ORD, nor upon the mock klaxons used by practical jokers. But Home Office officials do feel that more active support from clergymen[36] might help the government to guard against the comical element associated with ORD.

142. Another religious problem is the behaviour of a group of young clergymen who have come out openly in favour of SIFS (the Sex Is Fun Society). Whatever one may think about the propaganda put out by the SIF Society (and we have some comments to make in Part III of this report[37]), there is no doubt that the influence of this small group of church activists is bound to be disruptive, especially as many of them are self-declared homosexuals.

143. There is another group of moral pacemakers who, though they do not all belong to the same religious denomination, have collectively taken over the duty of acting as watchdogs. These earnest vigilants are to be found wherever there is a controversial moral problem, and ORD is no exception. They have resigned themselves to the restrictions of moral righteousness and their contribution is to make sure that everyone else will endure the same restraints. They may seem to be officious, but this is probably a cloak for a genuine desire to help people to avoid temptation.

---

[35] The reactor fits over the nipple and the lead runs to the ORD fitted under the breast. See Appendix A for the details.
[36] Not necessarily from the late Archbishop of Canterbury.
[37] Paragraphs 244–249.

144. It is this group of people, sometimes called the moral entrepreneurs, who are the first to see where others might be abusing the system or finding loopholes in the legal procedure. In the days when pornography was insufficiently controlled, they fearlessly attended the first nights of suspect films or plays, and bought doubtful books on the day they were published. Now that they have been relieved of some of these duties, they are able to devote more time to looking for faults in the operation of the Sexual Containment Act.

145. There are several examples of their indefatigable assiduity. They were the first to suggest that there were irregularities in the behaviour of the Referendaries. They have published a leaflet which suggests the proper denunciatory reaction to the activated klaxon; a simplified edition of this leaflet with illustrations has been distributed in all primary schools. They have campaigned for higher penalties for those who exceed the PNO and they advocate surgical castration for those who cannot be helped in any other way.

146. We understand why Ministers are uncertain how to deal with this group. They are the cause of much hostility and social alienation, partly because their press releases receive wide coverage although they are often inaccurate, and partly because their campaigns tend to make the general public discontented with the existing situation. On the other hand the government does not want to condemn their activities altogether because if ever the time came when it was necessary to reduce the PNO, it could rely upon this group for support.

147. Nevertheless the publicity given to these moral entrepreneurs has been sufficiently strident to induce MPs to ask several questions in the House and to wonder whether the Sexual Containment Act really is as effective as it is intended to be. There is the suspicion that some people are managing to evade the regulations and jealousy is on the increase. The unfortunate episode that led to the resignation of the late Archbishop of Canterbury was sparked off by an argument about exemptions. (Readers will remember that the Primate was visiting the faithful in the bars and clubs of Lambeth. In the course of a lively discussion, one woman said: 'It's easy for you to talk. You don't have to wear a fucking ORD.' We shall never know if the Archbishop had imbibed too well, or

whether he was trying to come down to the level of his flock. But everyone will agree that it was hardly the time or the place to pull up his cassock, pull down his underpants, and shout, 'See for yourselves.')

148. There are even rumours of night-long orgies in special rooms equipped with rays to make ORD inoperative. People gossip about an élite of sophisticated people who indulge in any amount of sex without appearing to be restricted in any way. Rumours like these make the headlines and then disappear and it is hard to tell if there is an element of truth in them. Consequently the government decided to set up a commission to review the workings of the Act since its inception three years ago. The next part of this report brings the situation up to date and discusses some of the problems that still remain.

PART III

# THE ACT IN OPERATION

## Introduction

149. This report differs in two ways from the earlier progress reports. First, it is to be made available to the public, who are invited to discuss our conclusions and make their views known to their members of Parliament. Second, our terms of reference are wider because we have been asked to take into account public attitudes to the Act and the whole concept of sexual containment. Accordingly we have divided this, the substantive part of the report, into six sections.

150. In the next section we will consider the advantages that have accrued from the Sexual Containment Act. In the following two sections we will examine the criticisms that have been levelled at the way the Act is working – first the economic problems and then the other complaints. Next we will look at the many suggestions that were sent to the Committee when its formation was announced. In the fifth section we will attempt to answer the most controversial question of all – who is to be exempt? In the last section we will consider the public attitudes to the Act and we will end by suggesting a few lessons that can be learnt from a study of the public will.

## Advantages

151. Much of the evidence we have received has affirmed that the Act has brought considerable benefits, but only a few specific instances have been mentioned. It may be that the advantages, though manifest to our witnesses, are not in the main either tangible or measurable.

152. The improvement most often mentioned is that people are now less obsessed with sex. It is said that if people are told they

cannot have more than a certain amount of sex, after a time they will stop thinking about it and start to do something else. Some go further than this and reaffirm Freud's theories on sublimation.[1] It is argued that the energy which cannot be used on sex will be diverted to other pursuits. It is assumed that the other pursuits will be more beneficial, but one cannot be absolutely sure of this.

153. It is instructive to look back at George Orwell's predictions for 1984, made thirty-five years ago, to see what relevance they have to the conditions of today. At one point in the story, Julia says:

> When you make love you're using up energy; and afterwards you feel happy and don't give a damn for anything. They can't bear you to think like that. They want you to be bursting with energy all the time. All this marching up and down and cheering and waving flags is simply sex gone sour.[2]

Elsewhere Orwell wrote: 'The Party was trying to kill the sex instinct, or, if it could not be killed, then to distort it and dirty it.' There are at least a few members in each of the eleven parties in today's House of Commons who hold similar views.

154. The professor of Behavioural Psychology at the Institute of Psychiatry has written: 'Sex is not necessary; it is a habit.'[3] The professor of Logic at Cambridge University said in a recent lecture that the Sexual Containment Act was good for morale. 'We may occasionally wish for more sex,' he continued, 'but our sex lives in the past were so dreary that a moment's pause makes us realise that we are really not missing much.' The Moderator of the General Assembly Church of Scotland has said: 'Ever since that happy day [when the Act received the Royal Assent], the boys run faster, the girls look prettier and the bairns have more colour in their cheeks.'

155. We acknowledge the strong feelings attached to these views and we recognize that it is not possible to verify these statements one way or the other. We think it should be said, however, that the theory of sublimation depends upon the idea that somewhere in the body there is a limited store of psychic energy and every time we experience a sexual emotion, such as passion or love, we are using up this valuable source of energy; if we do this too often –

[1] But see paragraph 11.
[2] Orwell, George, *Nineteen Eighty-Four*, Secker and Warburg, 1949.
[3] Westwood, G., *Bad Habits and What to Do About Them*. Penguin, 1979.

if, for example, we love too well – then the store of psychic energy will be exhausted. No physiological or psychological evidence has ever been found to support this theory.

156. Some moral leaders say that the greatest benefit bestowed by the Act is that it has rid us of improper sexual obligations – 'sex on demand' as they call it. In many books, plays and films it is assumed that when two people fall in love, they are obliged to have sexual intercourse together. Indeed the story line of many works of fiction depends upon this: the basic plot is that one of the pair who has fallen in love is already committed elsewhere and the main interest in the story is to see how these conflicting interests are resolved. In the real world it is easier to avoid these conflicts now that it is compulsory to wear ORD.

157. The partners in a modern marriage have a strong hold over one another. Each can keep count of the other's PNO and if there are any discrepancies an explanation can be demanded. This enables one partner in the marriage to keep a sharp eye on the extramarital activities of the other. Following a recent decision in court, it can now be regarded as legitimate grounds for divorce if (in the words of the judge) 'he or she knowingly and persistently fails to use his or her permitted number of orgasms with his or her spouse.'

158. It is probably true that there has been less infidelity and less premarital sex since the Act came into force. It seems likely that there is also less sexual intercourse between married couples, less homosexuality, less masturbation, less promiscuity, in fact, less sex. Presumably this also means there are fewer sexual deviations – less exhibitionism, less incest, less sadism, and less child molesting.[4]

159. There is also less pornography, but it is difficult to be sure whether this is due to the Sexual Containment Act. It is possible that the Act might have increased the demand for pornography, but if so, it is not being fulfilled. The legal restrictions on all books, pictures and performances are now so stringent that all forms of erotica have been driven underground. It is our impression that there is not much pornography being sold even in the back rooms of back streets. The desire to see it is not usually very powerful or compulsive and few people are going to risk the heavy prison

---

[4] But not less rape, as noted in paragraphs 123–4

sentences now being given for being in possession of an obscene article or for conspiring to commit an obscenity (eg possessing a book catalogue or a theatre ticket). As one of our witnesses said: 'Most people can take it or leave it and if they are forced to do without pornography, they'll happily do something else, like reading comics, drinking beer, eating sweets, watching sport, gambling, or any of the other simple things people like to do when they've got a moment to spare.'

160. If it is true, as the Cambridge professor of Logic has said, that our sex lives in the past were 'dreary'[5], it is possible that we do make a special effort to raise our standards now that we know the opportunities are limited. It is on this basis that some people argue that the Act has actually made sex more enjoyable: 'Sensible people,' they say, 'will not want to waste an orgasm by being slap-dash or offhand when they know they only have two a week.'

161. We have been surprised by the number of people who have told us that ORD has helped them to improve their sexual performance. We are at a loss to explain this, although there are many theories. One suggestion is that a steady electric current is set up by the metal in ORD making contact with the moist acid-containing skin of the male genitals and this gives the penis a mild shock which improves potency.[6] Another theory is that ORD provides some slight physical support for the man's genitals. It has been said that all penile rings induce 'agreeable erotic sensations, and hence boost morale, during the day'.[7] Yet another theory is that by adopting a special position during intercourse, ORD can be used to provide enhanced frictional stimulation for the female; readers of The Perfumed Garden[8] will know that no position is thought to be too awkward or too absurd.

---

[5] The professor used a rather inexact term, but there is evidence that many people were dissatisfied. It was reported in 1973, for example, that most people thought that everyone else's sex life was more exciting than their own – see Schofield, Michael, The Sexual Behaviour of Young Adults, Allen Lane, 1973.
[6] To test this claim, technicians at the government laboratories immersed ORD in a solution of urine; when ORD was connected to a sensitive volt-metre of 20,000 ohms resistance, a reading of 0.55 volts was recorded.
[7] Comfort, Alex (Ed.), The Joy of Sex, Quartet, 1974.
[8] Shaykh Nefzawi, The Perfumed Garden, Putman, 1964. It has been calculated, using modern computer methods, that there are 3,780 possible positions – Legman, G., Oragenitalism, Julian Press, 1969.

162. However, we believe that any improvement in sexual performance that is derived by wearing ORD is more likely to be due to psychological factors. We have already noted that some women enjoy wearing two ORDs and the 'adornment' factor may give a sexual boost to both male and female users. In a recent survey a surprisingly large number of men (21 per cent) and women (16 per cent) said that ORD had increased their sexual confidence; a smaller proportion said they would continue to wear it even if the recording mechanism had been switched off.[9] We have also received a report that a doctor in Zurich has imported a batch of ORDs and is using them in his clinic for treating men who are suffering from impotence; we have been told that the clinic is full and there is a long waiting list, but we have received no data which would enable us to evaluate this treatment.

163. Most of the information about ORD and improved sexual performance is anecdotal; a typical case history (no. 7) is given in Appendix B. The evidence is bound to be retrospective unless we are prepared to rely on the views of young people who start having sex before the age of 16. The government has turned down the application from the Marriage Guidance Association to conduct clinical trials on people having sexual intercourse with and without ORD. This caused disappointment in the Association as they had already prepared plans to convert their clinics and compiled a long list of volunteers willing to take part in the trials.

164. It is far better that people who have sexual difficulties should believe in ORD, which has no unfortunate side effects, rather than take alleged aphrodisiacs,[10] some of which are positively poisonous. For our part we are prepared to believe that a worthwhile number

---

[9] The respondents in this survey were a group of new users and it is always possible that the novelty will wear off in time.

[10] Throughout history man has diligently sought a miraculous aphrodisiac, so far with very little success. In the old days people believed in the magical principle that like cures like. For example, heart-shaped leaves were believed to cure heart disease, and the horn of a rhinoceros was thought to be of benefit to a man who could not get an erection. Even today there is demand for rhinoceros horns, ground up into a powder and taken by mouth. This is ineffective, but not toxic like cantharides (Spanish fly) or strychnine. The idea behind these poisonous substances is that it will cause irritation which will improve potency. Irritants do sometimes cause penile erections, but they also cause sickness and dysentery.

of men and women do find that ORD helps them with their sexual activities.

165. Like all the other advantages mentioned in this section, the evidence is neither as clear-cut nor as convincing as we would have wished. We are aware of the dangers of relying solely upon subjective evidence. The last Archbishop of Canterbury often said that sex is the cause of all our troubles and this illustrates the risks of relying too heavily upon personal experiences. We are forced to conclude that the advantages of ORD are more a matter of speculation than of calculation.

## Economic Criticisms

166. The criticism we have heard most frequently is that the administration of the Act is a very costly exercise. Some people are asking whether we can afford the luxury of sexual restraint during the present economic crisis. On the other hand, there are others who say that sexual containment is an indirect contribution to the gross national product.

167. The operation of the Act requires the employment of over 25,000 men and women. In addition to the network of Inspectorates all over the country, there is the large headquarters at Scarborough where they have taken over seven hotels, the training school at Colchester in the University of Essex buildings and the Inspector General's personal staff at his Mayfair office. To this must be added the Hormone Adjustment Clinics (HACs) in every Area Health Authority region and the five Sexual Retraining Centres (SRCs).

168. Originally the pay for Referendaries was below the national average; it was thought that it would not be difficult to recruit sufficient staff because the work had special attractions which were likely to appeal to a certain type of person; furthermore it does not require a particularly high level of intelligence to carry out the Referendary's tasks. But when ORD (Mark II) was introduced, it was necessary to man some Inspectorates twenty-four hours a day and the Union of Inspectors and Referendaries put in a claim for working unsocial hours. It will still be necessary to hold the Inspector's differentials as they deal with the recalcitrant cases and have the authority to levy on-the-spot fines.

169. The increasing manufacturing costs of ORD is another worry, but we would not like to recommend any economies in testing or quality control. We have already noted (paragraphs 105-6) the embarrassment caused to innocent subjects by faulty klaxons. One suggestion for saving money is omitting the klaxon in half the ORDs. As it will be impossible to tell which ORDs have the klaxon, the mere threat will be enough to stop most people from tampering with it. Those who make this suggestion use the analogy of the red burglar-alarm box prominently displayed on the outside of a building but not connected up to the electricity supply. We think it is a mistake to introduce this element of chance and we fear that some speculators will be tempted to risk entry by force.

170. But it is not really the expense of the Inspectorates nor the cost of ORD that really upsets people. It is the cost of staffing and running the HACs and SRCs. Spokesmen for the Carnival of White ask why a few moral degenerates should be such a burden on the taxpayer quite out of proportion to their numbers and to their value to society. Following their rally in Trafalgar Square in which many speeches were made about moral degenerates impoverishing the nation, the Home Secretary made a statement in the House of Commons: 'The Committee reviewing the operation of the Sexual Containment Act will be studying the procedures for dealing with imprudent sexual conduct. It is open to them to suggest changes in the law should they find this necessary.' Consequently we intend to deal with this matter in some detail.

171. The basic principle is that a subject who exceeds the permitted number of orgasms (PNO) needs to be helped with the control of the body and the mind. The control of the body is facilitated by attendance at the HAC. The control of the mind is re-learnt at the SRC. We have described the sex-steroid treatment provided at the HACs in part II (paragraphs 113-121). We will now outline the methods used at the SRCs and then consider whether there is any other procedure which can achieve similar results at less cost.

172. The treatment given at a SRC is sometimes called 'behaviour therapy'. This is a term used to describe a new psychotherapeutic method which is based on the assumption that neurotic behaviour is acquired and can be changed. Eysenck, one of the

leading figures in the field, postulates that 'neurotic symptoms are learned patterns of behaviour which for some reason or another are *unadaptive*.'[11] Behaviourists look upon sexual imprudence as being no more than faulty habits that have been picked up by accident. Current knowledge about the learning process has shown that not only can new habit patterns be acquired, but old habits can be eliminated, and this can be done clinically by what is known as 'aversion therapy'. The technique used in this kind of treatment is best described by summarizing a report from the *British Medical Journal*.

Treatment took place in a darkened room, and during it the patient was allowed no food or drink. At two-hourly intervals, she was given an injection of apomorphine – a drug which induces nausea and vomiting. On each occasion a strong light was shone on to a large piece of card on which were pasted photographs of nude men. The patient was asked to select one she found attractive, and it was suggested to her that she recreate her experience with a sexual partner. A tape recording was then played to her once every hour during the period of nausea. This explained the cause of her lack of self-control, suggesting it was a learned pattern reinforced by each sexual experience, and describing the adverse effects on her and its consequent social repercussions. The tape ended with words like 'sickening' and 'nauseating,' followed by the noise of someone vomiting. This accentuated the emetic effect of the apomorphine on the patient.

After 30 hours of this, the treatment was terminated, because the patient was in a very weak state. The next day the same type of treatment was restarted, but with another tape which was even more detailed about the effect the practices had on her and again ended with the words 'sickening' and 'nauseating'. This went on until she again became too weak, this time after 32 hours.

The following night, the patient was awakened every 2 hours and a record was played which congratulated her and explained in optimistic terms what would be accomplished if her sexual drive could be controlled. The following morning she was al-

---

[11] Eysenck, H. J. (ed.), *Behaviour Therapy and the Neuroses*, Pergamon, 1960.

lowed up and about. The treatment continued in concentrated form for five more days. For the rest of the month it was only necessary to give treatment once a week. She was allowed to mix with other patients and a careful watch was kept on her conduct for signs of a possible relapse.

By the time she left the Sexual Retraining Centre, her whole demeanor has altered. Her relatives describe her as 'a new woman', and her relationships with them as wholly satisfactory and better than at any time in her life. She herself has felt no strong sexual urge since treatment, whereas previously she had been troubled by sexual fantasies throughout every day. She has tried kissing once or twice since she left the Centre but still regards this with a certain amount of revulsion. She no longer finds it necessary to lie or spend beyond her means. She feels generally at ease and happier than at any time since her childhood, and describes the treatment as 'fantastically successful' and comments on its swiftness.

173. The treatment given at SRCs varies according to the needs of the patient and also depends upon the moral outlook of the therapist. Some therapists hold the theory that it is better that the patient be completely devoid of sexual interest when he leaves the SRC, but others think this may make it more difficult to adjust to outside conditions, especially if he is married. Another variation is that some therapists do not use prerecorded tapes during the treatment but believe it is more effective if they personally subject the patient to moralistic harangues and derision.

174. Therapists are turning away from the use of emetics because it is not easy to control the severity of the vomiting. The use of electric shocks avoids this difficulty and is probably more effective since the speed and certainty with which pain follows the sexual stimulus is more important than the severity of the punishment.

175. Treatment at the SRCs does not consist only of aversion therapy. In a number of cases 'positive conditioning' is used in combination with punishments. Sometimes a patient is given a degree of control over his own shock therapy by pressing a button which causes the removal of a sexually stimulating picture from the screen; if he is quick enough, he may avoid getting the electric shock. Thus he can develop a positive feeling of having some say in what happens to him.

176. The administrators of the SRCs are aware of the need to economize. In order to cut down on the expense of employing more therapists, they have arranged for trusted inmates to administer the electric shocks to other patients receiving aversion therapy. Professor Milgram's research has indicated that many of the inmates are perfectly prepared to undertake this work.[12]

177. The administrators are most anxious to avoid a 'clockwork orange' image at the SRCs. The conditions are made as comfortable as possible and in between treatment sessions patients are free to read, watch TV or play ping-pong. Although the term 'corrective therapy' is used in the Act, treatment at the SRCs is always referred to as 'behaviour modification' and though most of the inmates are offenders sent there by the courts, they are known as 'patients' and the staff often call them by their Christian names.

178. Unfortunately it is our duty to report that there have been a number of fatalities at the SRCs due to heart failure, poisoning by the emetic and electrocution. In their evidence the Institute of Behaviourists claim that the mortality rate is surprisingly low considering the numbers passing through the Centres and the pressures of overwork suffered by the therapists. We are not qualified to express an opinion about this, but we understand that of the 36 who died during aversion therapy last year, 2 of them were volunteers (ie not sent by the court) and we find this regrettable.

179. Even more distressing than the mortality rate is the low success rate. Unfortunately there have been far too few careful

---

[12] Milgram set up an experiment in which volunteers were asked to administer electric shocks to an experimental subject whenever he made a mistake performing an allocated task. The more mistakes he made, the more severe the shocks. The volunteer was told that beyond a certain point the shocks would be very painful and those at the top of the ascending scale of severity were positively dangerous. What the volunteer did not know was that the experimental subject was an actor pretending to receive the shocks. Milgram found that a high proportion of volunteers continued to give more and more severe shocks every time the actor made a mistake, even if he was screaming with pain and begging him to stop; towards the end of the experiment the actor would be quite silent, pretending to have passed out. Even then some of the volunteers continued to give (what they thought were) severe shocks everytime he failed to complete the allocated task. When questioned later, they said they were only obeying instructions and could not be held responsible as it was not their experiment. Milgram, Stanley, *Obedience to Authority*, Tavistook, 1974.

follow-up studies after attendance at a SRC. In one study of 167 patients, 88 per cent had not relapsed after six months and 12 per cent remained sexually imprudent. But a further follow-up two years later found that 47 per cent had relapsed and 9 per cent had been sent back to the SRC three or more times. If these figures are at all representative, then over 330,000 of the three-quarters of a million who have attended the SRCs are still finding it difficult to control their sexual drives.

180. These are very large numbers and it is understandable that the National Scopophilic Association are protesting vigorously about the unfair financial burden this places on the sexually restrained. For many years psychoanalysts have been saying that behaviour therapy is unlikely to be successful because it does not even attempt to attack the root of the problem; if you block the outward symptom, they would say, then the basic neurosis must come out in some other way, probably in a far more complex and anti-social way leading to a complete breakdown. Even the behaviourists agree that it is impossible to guarantee that any reduction in sexual activity will be maintained. The treatment seems to depend on periodic reinforcement and, of course, it is very expensive to continue to provide this.

181. Most of the reports on corrective therapy note a general improvement of social attitudes in the patient. This general all-round improvement is reported with satisfaction by the therapists, but it fills us with misgivings. Anthropologists have often noted that the activities of African witch-doctors more often result in general improvement rather than a specific cure of a particular ailment. In many ways behaviour therapy is too closely akin to 'thought reform', or what is more often known as 'brain washing'. In fact it is a method of imposing one person's will upon another and it would assist our peace of mind if we could find some other method of treatment which is more effective but less ominous and less costly.

182. We do not think that psychoanalysis or any other form of psychiatric treatment can provide the solution we seek. The steroid treatment given in the HACs has been more successful than behaviour therapy and this has led us to look at other forms of physical treatment.

E

183. One possibility is the surgical destruction of a small area of the hypothalamus, which is said to act as a 'sex behaviour centre'. This is of potential interest because it may indicate that there are some cases of sexual misconduct due to defects in small areas of the brain which doctors have not yet been able to diagnose. This supposition is supported by the fact that if a certain small portion of an animal's brain is artificially damaged it results in 'sexual perversity'. Animal experiments in government laboratories have shown that sexual behaviour and capacity can be affected by the administration of other substances; for example, 'rabbits given para-chlorphenylalanine will mount cats regardless of being scratched.'[13]

184. This kind of treatment has met with only partial success so far, but the potentialities are fearsome. We have been told that government technicians are also working on a chastity belt for males. We do not understand why this device should be designed particularly for men, unless officials at the Department of Health and Social Security think that the historical models worn in the Middle Ages are still perfectly adequate for the protection of women.

185. But by far the most popular solution, advocated by the Categorical Society and many others, is castration. The real problem is that hormone compounds given at HACs lose their effect if not taken regularly and subjects who attend SRCs are likely to relapse. The Categorical Society believes that it is giving the subject too much responsibility to leave the control of his sexual drive in his own hands. Patients fail to continue with the treatment and disappear for weeks on end. There have been clamorous demands at Carnival of White rallies for a more permanent solution.

186. In their evidence the National Scopophilic Association have pointed out the high cost of running the network of HACS: 'The cost of the drugs, the necessity for regular visits, the salaries of doctors and auxiliary workers and other expenses add up to a formidable sum. Why should the taxpayer have to pay this colossal bill for dealing with sexual psychopaths and moral degenerates?

---

[13] Cauthery, Philip and Cole, Martin, *The Fundamentals of Sex*, Allen, 1971.

In one sense, hormone treatment is a form of chemical castration. It would be much simpler to remove their gonads. To cut is cheaper.'

187. In Sweden and Finland the courts have power to order the compulsory castration of certain offenders. In Denmark sex criminals who have been committed to prison for an indefinite period may obtain their release more quickly by 'volunteering' to undergo castration.[14] In the United States, judges sometimes grant probation on condition that the sex offender agrees to this operation.[15] The Director of a Kansas State Penitentiary argues that castration has made 330 males at his institution more stable and peaceful, less a 'social menace'.[16] A former warden of San Quentin prison has said that the Californian criminals who submitted to castration usually thank the doctor for performing the operation.

188. However, we have decided not to recommend surgical castration for those who require treatment at HACs or SRCs. We are not convinced that such an irreversible step can be justified. Bremer[17] evaluated the results of castration in men, 102 of whom were sex offenders; he concluded that only 22 of the sex offenders would have relapsed if they had not been castrated. Furthermore castration appears to have very variable consequences. It does not always abolish sexual appetites. There are reports of castrated adults who continue to lead an active sex life, although they are sterile. The nervous reflexes governing ejaculation can continue unimpaired, even without testicles. Another disadvantage is that castration is normally only used on men, although in Paris in the 1880s women were subjected to cauterization of the clitoris as a cure for excessive masturbation.

189. For these reasons we do not recommend that castration should be one of the optional treatments for the sexually imprudent. There are indications that hormone therapy will be improved and

[14] Sturup, G. K., 'Sex Offences: the Scandinavian Experience', *Law and Contemporary Problems*, 23, 361–375, 1960.
[15] Slovenko, R., *Sexual Behaviour and the Law*, Thomas, 1965.
[16] Karlen, Arno, *Sexuality and Homosexuality*, MacDonald, 1971.
[17] Bremer, Johan, *Asexualization: A Follow-up Study of 244 Cases*, Macmillan, 1959.

refined in the not too distant future. For example, there are techniques now being used of implanting steroid compounds into the body which means that the patient need only visit the clinic once or twice a year. It seems less likely that there will be dramatic improvements in the surgical techniques of castration.

190. We have placed our views on hormone adjustment, sexual retraining and castration under the heading of economic criticisms because this is the aspect that seems to concern most members of Parliament. We are well aware that there are considerable ethical problems but politicians, and the public they represent, appear to be less worried by these.[18] We think this is a pity. We would like to urge more vigilance, but we understand that the price of liberty is less important than the cost of living in the present economic climate.

## Other Criticisms

### (a) Sex Without Orgasm

191. The groups that are in favour of castration are also deeply concerned about the increasing tendency to indulge in sexual activities without reaching orgasm. They see this as a loophole in the Act and demand that something be done about it. They allege that it is physically harmful to become sexually excited without reaching and passing the point of orgasm. We have made enquiries about this and have found that many doctors support this view. But the doctors were not very specific when we asked exactly which parts of the body were harmed and how many cases of this kind they had treated.[19]

192. We have also heard reports about a special school recently opened in Oxford Street which promises to teach men how to have sexual intercourse without an orgasm. We understand their methods

[18] All our witnesses in favour of castration answered our question about the ethical problems by insisting that even the most repugnant acts can be justified if the prosperity of the State is at risk.
[19] It is often said that it is harmful for a man to allow the penis to go flaccid without ejaculating, but the medical evidence is confused. The Oneida Community in New York systematically practised *coitus reservatus* without any reported harmful results. In ancient Taoist doctrine it is said to be spiritually and physically beneficial for a man to retain his semen and to allow 'his sperm to flow into his bloodstream to nourish his brain.'

are based on the techniques used to cure premature ejaculation. The instructor (usually, but not necessarily a woman) masturbates the client to the point of orgasm and then stops until the desire has dissipated; then she starts again, and so on until he has learnt to delay ejaculation indefinitely. If the client gets too excited, she places a thumb on the frenulum,[20] one finger on the corona[21] and another on the shaft of his penis and squeezes. This stops the man's desire to ejaculate. It may also give him a pain in his testicles. For an extra fee the wife or girl friend can attend the course and learn to practise these techniques on her man (see case history no. 8 in Appendix B).

193. We have also received complaints that an undisclosed number of men are in a semi-erect state for long periods of the day. There is a racial element in these complaints because in nearly all cases the allegation has been about black men. It is said that the penis of a black man tends to appear larger than the penis of a man belonging to the white or yellow races[22] and this may be the cause of the misunderstanding; it may be that the complainant (usually a housewife from a district where there are not many immigrants) has caught a glimpse of a black man's penis and, because of its unusual size, has jumped to the conclusion that it is not as flaccid as it should be.

194. The situation is confused still further by another complaint we have received. This is about a particular clothing manufacturer who is advertising trousers especially shaped for men who maintain an erection for long periods. We have had a selection of these trousers sent to us and we find upon examination that notwithstanding the wording of the advertisements the trousers are padded

---

[20] The *frenulum* is the bridge of skin on the undersurface of the penis uniting the glans penis with the foreskin.

[21] The *corona* is the rim of the glans penis.

[22] We are informed by people who have made a life-long study of the matter that this is a misapprehension. Dr Jacobus (*L'Ethnologie du Sens Genitale*, Liseux, 1893) noted that the penis of the Caucasian European and the Semite Arab 'is short and small because it becomes more flaccid than the detumescent penis of the Negro which remains semi-erect. But the erect genital member of the Caucasian or Semite rivals that of the Negro for size and length.' Sir Richard Burton (*Personal Narrative of a Pilgrimage to El-Medina and Mecca*, Bell, 1898) made a similar observation and remarked that 'the African's member is long, thick and flabby, and lengthens very little from a state of quiescence to that of erection.'

so as to give the *appearance* of an erection, which is not quite the same thing.

195. We cannot offer any practical suggestions as to how these criticisms can be met. Clearly these moral entrepreneurs feel it to be the duty of every citizen to avoid circumstances that may be stimulating. They demand that all sexual excitement should be, if not stopped, at least recorded and controlled. But they know that ORD will only record orgasms and we do not see how it can be modified so that it will measure the level of sexual stimulation. In any case we are not convinced that those who enjoy sensuous pleasures without insisting upon an orgasmic climax are necessarily mistaken. We are inclined to look with favour upon the French philosophy that sometimes it is better to journey than to arrive.

*(b) Long Term Effects*

196. A different section of the community is worried about the possible long term effects of wearing ORD. Only a few are concerned about the physical consequences of having ORD attached to their persons. Some subjects feel uncomfortable at the outset because it is such a new experience, but they soon get used to wearing it. The instructions about cleaning and the regular visits to the Inspectorate guard against the dangers of inflammation or skin rash.

197. The area of controversy concerns the possible physical or psychological effects of limiting the number of orgasms. Thousands of books and magazine articles have been written about the consequences of having too much or too little sexual activity. Some people write as if we all have a limited sex ration and a profligate libertine will be debilitated before middle age. Others have suggested that men and women who continue to have sexual experiences into old age are healthier in mind and body. Unfortunately this mass of material is not well documented and it is difficult to draw any conclusions.

198. Not much can be learnt from the biographies of people who went to one extreme or the other. Well known rakes in history usually ended up by being riddled with the pox; that may have been their just deserts, but it cannot be regarded as the direct consequence of too much sex. The study of the lives of holy men is no more instructive. Of course we cannot assume that celibacy and

chastity are the same thing. The history of Christendom suggests that the most dogmatic personalities are those who are first licentious and then ascetic. This may help to explain the assertions made by members of the Categorical Society, but it does not help us very much.

199. It is, of course, impossible to be absolutely sure that the effects of the Sexual Containment Act will not be physically or mentally disabling in the distant future. Within the next decade we expect the sexologists to make a pronouncement about the optimum number of orgasms in a week, a month and a year. We cannot be sure that the optimum will not be higher or lower than the present PNO of 27 a quarter. All we can say is that we have no reason to suspect that ORD has any deleterious effects in the long run.

200. It is worth noting that dire warnings about possible long term harmful effects is a favourite stratagem of those who do not like change. Most innovations are mistrusted at first; so when a novel idea or a new product is found to be of manifest benefit to the community, it is up to the prohibitors to produce the evidence that its harmful effects in the long run outweigh the immediate benefits. Even with medicines, although tests are made and precautions taken, it is always possible that some of them may turn out to be harmful, but this possibility by itself is not sufficient reason to ban them; if it were, it would be necessary to prohibit nearly all the recent medical discoveries which continue to be used successfully against physical and mental ill-health. Doomwatchers must produce the evidence before sanctions can be justified. Does anyone really know about the long term effects of, for example, rumbustious rock on youthful ears, city air on our lungs, frozen food on our digestion, or vaginal deodorants on our pudenda?

## (c) Political Implications

201. One other criticism has been voiced recently and this is the fear that the Sexual Containment Act might be used for political purposes. The complaint was first heard last year soon after the Prime Minister announced that an extra orgasm would be allowed on the Queen's birthday. The Prime Minister has all along insisted that she intended this to be no more than a gesture of loyalty towards Her Gracious Majesty. This may be so, but the announce-

ment was misinterpreted by some people because it came just a week before the important by-election at Ashford.

202. It will be remembered that the Liberal Party in their manifesto at the last general election promised to increase the PNO. Sir David Butler and other psephologists have concluded that this political manoeuvre did not significantly increase the Liberal vote. This may be because the public feel instinctively that sexual containment should not become a party political issue, or it may be that there is not much demand for an increase in the PNO.

**Proposals and Other Pressures**

*(a) Introduction*

203. All interested organizations were invited to submit their proposals and a general invitation was issued in the press for individuals to send us their views. We are bound to say that we were rather disappointed with the response. Fewer than 30 organizations and only 17 individuals sent memoranda or letters. Much of the evidence we received came from organizations which were already committed to a public policy towards the Act. We have considered their proposals in the previous paragraphs of this report. In this section we deal with the memoranda and letters that advocate less familiar lines of thought.

*(b) The Optimum Number of Orgasms*

204. We were not surprised to find that many of our witnesses had much to say about the number of orgasms that should be permitted. One representative of the Carnival of White suggested that the PNO should be reduced each year until eventually it was zero. She continued: 'All sex, even within monogamous marriage, has become an unnecessary luxury. Now that women can be artificially inseminated for reproductive purposes, there is no longer any good reason for wasting energy on sexual intercourse which is tiring, tedious, inefficient and unhygienic'.

205. The Institution of Psychiatrists are also critical of the PNO. They maintain that there are wide variations in sexual requirements and only psychiatrists are able to judge the amount of sex each individual needs; whereas an annual quota of 108 orgasms may well be

satisfactory for some people, others would need at least 150, and most certainly there were others who should not have more than 50.

206. The Institute sent a complicated proposal which can be summarized simply by stating that psychiatrists should be employed to interview and test all subjects at least once every quinquennium and they alone would have the power to raise or lower the PNO of each individual. The Institute admitted that there were not enough qualified psychiatrists at present to make this plan a practical proposition, but they proposed a considerable increase in their salaries which would make the profession more attractive, thereby assisting recruitment which would alleviate the shortage.

207. We have also received evidence from the Campaign for Homosexual Equality (CHE) in direct conflict with this. They maintain that the psychiatrists had too much influence during the original consultations which took place before the PNO was fixed and, as a result, a wholly inaccurate view of typical sexual behaviour has been taken. Furthermore, they claim that psychiatrists do not know much about normal sexuality because they generalize from information obtained from patients in their clinics, most of whom suffer from serious personality problems; not only do psychiatrists have a warped view of normal sexual behaviour, but they have very little success in curing those who come to them with sexual problems.

208. While wishing to avoid the question of what is normal and abnormal sexual behaviour, we are inclined to agree with at least the last part of the evidence from CHE. We think that in the past too much weight has been given to the opinions of psychiatrists, most of whom tend to be lax in providing evidence to support their declarations. Too often the only source of their information is the records kept by individual psychiatrists and inferences drawn from these records are hazardous at best. We must reject the plan put forward by the Institute of Psychiatrists because we are not convinced that they do in fact know much more about individual sexual requirements than anyone else.

209. We are not at liberty to disclose who was invited to the conferences that took place prior to the inception of ORD, but we can confirm that a large number of moral authorities were consulted, including psychiatrists, sociologists, anthropologists, poli-

ticians from all eleven parties, and religious leaders of many faiths. The British Humanist Association has commented that a celibate priest should be the last person to be asked to advise on the PNO, but the Vatican's representative in the UK has put quite a different view. 'The fact that a Roman Catholic priest is unmarried does not necessarily mean that he is uninformed about sexual matters,' he writes. 'A priest may not have much practical experience of hetero-sexual union, but in other ways he may have gained considerable expertise.'

210. We have received a strongly-worded memorandum from the Women's Organization claiming that women are entitled to a higher PNO than men. During sexual intercourse a woman might well have 3 or 4 orgasms, while a man has only 1. Each orgasm is recorded, so one sexual act may count as 3 or 4 for a woman but only as one for a man. So, it is argued, if a woman is to be allowed to have sexual intercourse as often as a man, her PNO should be 3 or 4 times greater. Their written evidence ends as follows: 'As it is obvious that nature intended the human female to have more orgasms than the human male, it is unnatural, unfair and inhuman for both of them to be allocated the same quota.'

211. When the Committee heard oral evidence, Lady Alicia Featherstonhaugh, who was one of the representatives of the Women's Organization, was asked if she would agree to keeping the PNO at the same level for women but reducing it for men by a third or a quarter. She replied that this may well be a solution from the point of view of the male-orientated Committee, but she, speaking personally, would find it quite unsatisfactory.

212. We do not dispute the facts on which the women's pro-posals are based, but more than one conclusion can be drawn. Modern sex research shows that the average male orgasm rarely lasts for more than 6 seconds, and after that he is not normally capable of further orgasms until he has had a rest.[23] The period

---

[23] Although a few men below the age of 30 have been observed (by in-vestigators at the Health Education Council's Research Unit) to ejaculate 4 or 5 times in half an hour, each experience is a separate orgasm, because on each occasion the urethral bulb distends and then immediately contracts after the seminal fluid has been expelled. Males over the age of 30 soon lose the ability to ejaculate so frequently.

of rest required (the refractory period) depends on several factors, mainly age, health and ardour (in that order of importance). But a woman can have several orgasms in rapid succession. Even after 3 or 4 orgasms the female has a much shorter refractory period than the male and she can soon respond again to sexual stimuli.

213. One possible interpretation of these facts is that sexual constraint is more necessary for women than for men. In any case we are most reluctant to re-introduce a double standard of sexual behaviour. For too many years it was assumed that men could be profligate and promiscuous while women had to remain pure and faithful. We now know that the sexual response of the female is just as strong as the male's. It would be a pity if this Committee now made recommendations that were divisive. A better solution would be to persuade both men and women that they can, with practice, choose the moment (within limits) when they reach the climax of their sexual activities.

214. We have reported in some detail on the evidence of psychiatrists, homosexuals and women, and we hope this will encourage further discussion. There is no compelling reason why the PNO should always be 108 per annum, but we have not yet heard any convincing evidence that persuades us to recommend that it should be other than it is.

## (c) The Starting Age

215. The pressure groups that advocate castration in order to avoid wasting the taxpayer's money on moral degenerates have also conducted a lively campaign to lower the age at which it becomes compulsory to wear ORD. From one point of view this is inconsistent because it would be a large additional expense to fit ORDs to children under the age of 16. These organizations do not normally think it is important to pursue a consistent logical policy, but the protection of youth has always been one of their main objectives.

216. The arbitrary determination of an age level below which certain activities become unlawful is bound to be controversial. The age of consent for sexual intercourse is 16; the legal age of majority is 18; homosexuals have to wait until they are 21. The arguments in favour of lowering the compulsory age for wearing ORD are that many boys and girls have sexual intercourse before

their sixteenth birthday and some young people seem to be determined to have as much sex as possible before restrictions are placed
on their activities.

217. In our discussions the following arguments have been advanced against lowering the age limit:

(1) It would be very inconsistent to have an age lower than
the age of consent. The age of 15, 14 or even 12, as some have
proposed, would be just as arbitrary and the only valid reason
for lowering the age would be if the age of consent were also
lowered.

(2) Inspectors and Referendaries would, in theory at least,
be aiding and abetting an offence by fitting ORD to a person
below the age of consent.

(3) The breasts of some girls at a lower age would be under-
developed and it would be difficult to fit ORD.

(4) It might encourage some boys and girls to have sex who
might not have done so if they were not wearing ORD.

(5) It would be an unnecessary expense because it is still true
that a large number of adolescents do not have sexual intercourse before they are 16.

218. Research results[24] have shown that the number of people who
have sexual intercourse when they are below the age of consent is
not as large as people fear. Nevertheless puberty starts for girls at
about 11–13 on average and around 12–14 for boys. Adolescents
are now taller, heavier and physically more developed in every
way, so it is scarcely surprising that some of them will want to
experiment before their sixteenth birthday. The practical reason
for trying to stop them in the past was to avoid the tragedy of
becoming an adolescent mother or the hazards of an adolescent
abortion. This still happens sometimes because a girl is shy about
getting contraceptive advice.

219. We do not think anything is to be gained by lowering the
age at which it becomes compulsory to fit ORD. It would be more
helpful if our resources were used to close the gap that still exists
between the moment when a girl first has sexual intercourse and

---

[24] Schofield, Michael, *The Sexual Behaviour of Young People*, Longmans,
1965.

the time when she starts to use contraceptives; this probably means that girls should know all about birth control and should be encouraged to use contraceptives before their first experience of sexual intercourse.

## (d) Promiscuity

220. The same pressure groups are worried by the extent of promiscuity. Our impression is that there is less promiscuity since the Act was passed simply because people do not want to waste orgasms on unknown and untried strangers. But the Categorical Society feels that the government made a serious blunder when they introduced ORD without incorporating some device which would act as an impediment against promiscuous activities. Accordingly they have employed a firm of design engineers to produce an ingenious device which is based on the principle of the plug and socket. The male wears an instrument which resembles a bung and this fits into an opening on a device which is worn by the female. The apparatus is designed to work like a lock and key. The man's projection will only plug into his wife's socket and no one else's. If he or his wife attempts to have sexual intercourse with anyone else, the device projecting from the male would make coitus very uncomfortable.

221. This apparatus is not, of course, a component of ORD but a completely separate appliance, worn on the penis in the case of the male. The objective is sexual particularism, not containment, and the relevance to the workings of this Act is not easily perceived. Furthermore the apparatus is unreliable. When tests were made on volunteers (not, we are informed, members of the Categorical Society), the appliance jammed on several occasions and it sometimes took a locksmith 40 minutes to prise the couple apart.

## (e) Premarital Credits

222. The same organizations were disappointed that the Act had not been successful in stopping premarital sexual intercourse. Indeed the National Scopophilic Association has pointed out, with some justification and much acerbity, that the Act had, if anything, encouraged young people to have sexual intercourse before marriage; from the age of 16 they have 27 orgasms allowed every 13 weeks

and many of them feel under some obligation to use every one; in some circles a youth is the object of scorn and innuendo if it becomes known that he or she has not used the full quota of orgasms. In order to counteract this situation, the Association has submitted a scheme which is certainly more viable and elegant than the proposal described in the previous paragraph.

223. When a subject reports to the Inspectorate and the ORD is removed for servicing, the recording mechanism is invariably turned back to zero. If the subject has had fewer than 27 orgasms during that quarter, the unused ones cannot be added to the PNO for the next quarter. If, for example, a girl is ill or her husband is away for a few weeks and she has only had 21 orgasms, she cannot expect an allowance of 33 (27+6) during the next period. Many people think this is unfair and the National Scopophilic Association think this discourages young people from remaining chaste. So they have produced this idea of a premarital credit scheme.

224. They suggest that the National Computer could be wired to every Inspectorate and programmed to keep a record of every unused orgasm, which becomes a credit. After every visit to the Inspectorate, the subject's credits would be added to his record and his PNO for the next quarter amended accordingly. This would be much fairer on those who, for one reason or another, are abstemious for a period; for example, those who are ill, tired, away from home or giving up sex for Lent. It would encourage the young to be careful and thrifty. It would also counteract the present unfortunate tendency to marry at an early age. Most important of all, it would persuade young people that they are not missing something if they do not have sex before marriage; indeed, say the NSA, 'a girl could look upon her credits as a dowry.'

225. We are interested in this scheme and think it merits further discussion, but we are not going to recommend its adoption at this stage because there are some weighty arguments against it. For one thing, it will be expensive to administer; this is a serious disadvantage because many people, including the sponsors of this scheme, are complaining about the operating costs of this Act.

226. Furthermore the underlying assumption lends credibility to the already too prevalent feeling that orgasms are like wages – assets to be disposed of at will; this is surely against the spirit as

well as the letter of the Act. For example, a girl who does not get married until she is 26[25] and has remained a virgin would have a credit of over 1,000 orgasms; this is bound to have some effects on the attitude of the bride, not to mention the bridegroom, who may be encouraged or intimidated.

227. The credit scheme is unlikely to promote the romantic ideal as an integral part of love and marriage. It is instructive to imagine the scene when a man proposes to a girl, adding by way of inducement that he has a credit of 50 orgasms, but the girl replies that she has over 300 so she does not think they will make a very suitable match. Even if they were so in love that they were determined to get married despite this disparity, those extra 250 credits would become a quarterly reminder to the wife and a recurrent threat for the husband.

228. Another objection to the credit scheme is that people will become confused if their PNO varies throughout the year. Indeed we have received evidence that some subjects get confused as things are at present. Many subjects who exceed their PNO say they have lost count and promise the Referendary to make up for it during the following quarterly period. It will be remembered that when the original calculation was made, an extra orgasm was added to the twice weekly ration over the 13 week period and this was intended as a concession for the careless and confused. We do not think it would be appropriate to make any more concessions of this kind.

229. We are aware that several enterprising firms have put special calendars and press-button calculators on the market and these should help people to keep a note of the number of orgasms they have expended; one model has a small light and a clip that fits over the bedhead so that a note can be made immediately after intercourse without getting out of bed.

230. Even with this *aide-mémoire*, we do not think this proposal is felicitous. If a credit scheme were introduced, there would soon be a demand for a debit scheme along similar lines; subjects would

---

[25] Twenty-six is still quite a common age for a girl to marry even though teenage weddings have become more popular now that young people are wearing ORD.

exceed their PNO and then would want to redeem it by instalments, like a Barclaycard.

231. We have not overlooked the fact that only unmarried subjects can accumulate credits. The National Scopophilic Association's proposal would not allow married subjects to receive credits because 'this would encourage infidelities when one of the partners was absent, indisposed, pregnant, or perfidious.' But if the single are allowed to build up credits and the married are forbidden to do this, then many subjects will decide to live together without getting married. This would constitute a threat to family life and the sanctity of marriage. Clearly, this is not what the proposers of the scheme have in mind. This leaves the National Scopophilic Association in their customary position of being somewhat embarrassed when their own policies are taken seriously.

### (f) Tourists and Foreigners

232. The arrival of foreign visitors was one of the early problems that arose soon after ORD was introduced and we have discussed some of the difficulties in Part II. We have recently received a memoranda from the National Flag which suggests a rather different policy. They propose that tourists should be allowed into Britain without being fitted with ORD from October to April; one of the problems of the tourist trade is that it tends to be concentrated into the summer months and this special inducement would help to spread the influx of tourists over the less popular winter period. Although this concession would appear to encourage sexual indulgence, the National Flag declares this need not be a cause for concern; if the tourists attempt to involve British subjects in their sexual activities, the Sexual Containment Act provides a hidden restraint, for few loyal subjects are likely to want to waste orgasms on casual encounters with foreigners who may well be diseased. 'But if the tourists wish to copulate with one another,' the memorandum continues, 'this is a matter of indifference, for it is not in our interests to prevent foreigners from demeaning themselves.'

233. It has been our experience that chauvinism and moralism are often found together. Quite apart from the sentiments expressed in the memorandum from the National Flag, there are

differing opinions about the attitudes of tourists. As we have noted[26] some people think that the prospect of being fitted with ORD arouses salacious curiosity and has stimulated the tourist trade, but others think that foreigners would prefer to visit Britain when it is not compulsory to wear ORD.

234. We require more information. We must await the results of the psychological studies being carried out at the Pudsey Polytechnic where they have set out to discover what, if any, are the inner satisfactions to be obtained from wearing ORD.

## (g) Independent Tribunals

235. The National Council for Civil Liberties has put forward a strong case for the establishment of independent tribunals. No matter how fair and thorough the investigation is under the present complaints procedure, it is always one Inspector judging another and this inevitably leaves room for accusations of bias or whitewashing. The NCCL proposes that an independent tribunal, consisting of one layman, one laywoman (preferably with sexual experience) and a chairperson from the legal profession, be given powers to:

(1) Enquire into allegations of serious infringements of the Code of Practice by Inspectors and Referendaries.
(2) Hear appeals against the decisions of Inspectors in other cases of alleged malpractices.

236. We were alarmed by the reports of a recent case in which an Inspector was arrested for bribery while he was investigating a similar case himself.[27] Equally distressing was the report of another case in which an Inspector was accused of persuading a subject to have a number of extra orgasms and then fining him for exceeding his PNO. During the investigation it was revealed that this Inspector had previously been asked to resign from the drug squad of the Metropolitan Police because he was suspected of planting cannabis on innocent travellers going to a pop festival. We are assured by Home Office officials that promotion in the corps does not depend upon the number of subjects apprehended for exceeding

---

[26] Paragraph 129.
[27] Case history no. 9 in Appendix B.

F

the PNO, but they have disclosed that Inspectors receive a small commission on fines: 'We do not think this leads to malpractices,' they told us. 'It is an accepted mode of incentive used to motivate salesmen, shop assistants and others.'

237. Rudeness seems to have abated since the new training programme was instituted, but we have received complaints about Referendaries taking bribes or homosexual liberties. These are clearly infringements of the Code of Practice and the dispute is usually about who is telling the truth. But there are other cases not covered by the Code and the argument in favour of an independent tribunal is stronger when these borderline cases occur. We have had one report[28] about an Inspector who introduced the wife of one of his subjects to another man – 'with the best of intentions,' he claimed, 'because they both had orgasms to spare.' Another case involved a Referendary who talked too freely in his local pub and divulged confidential details which he had obtained at the Inspectorate; one married woman complained because everyone in the village seemed to know that her husband never had any orgasms recorded on his ORD, but she always had precisely the same number as her close friend, a divorcee who lived three doors away.

238. At present there is no right of appeal against the Inspector's decisions. Many of the protests come from subjects who say the reading on ORD must be wrong. We doubt if an appeal procedure would be very helpful in these cases because in a conflict between machine and memory it is almost impossible to prove the machine is wrong. But Inspectors are permitted to make on-the-spot fines up to £250 and we think there is a real danger of bribery here. We realize that the Union of Inspectors and Referendaries[29] will not take kindly to this observation, but case histories 1–3, 9 and 10 are examples of the kind of pressures that can be put upon a subject and there may well be others that never come to light. In some cases it is not the fine but the fear of publicity that worries the subject and this raises the possibility of blackmail.

239. In their evidence the Union maintains that *only* an Inspector has the knowledge to investigate another Inspector. 'Only

---

28 Case history no. 10 in Appendix B.
29 Now part of Lord Jenkins's ASTMS.

he is aware of the difficulties, temptations and tricks of the trade. Only an Inspector with wide experience will know how to combat the hundred and one ruses that subjects will try on in the hope of getting a few more orgasms. Outside investigators would not have the necessary experience and therefore would be easily deceived by the unscrupulous subject. An Inspector can spot a discrepancy in a subject's story because he has heard it all before, many times.' In addition the Union of Inspectors and Referendaries say that they need legal protection from trivial complaints in the same way that the police can charge a man under the Criminal Law Act 1967 for knowingly wasting a policeman's time. Despite these weighty words we still have doubts about the effectiveness of Inspectors investigating other Inspectors without any reference or appeal to an independent outside body.

240. An independent tribunal could also deal with complaints about the administration inside HACs and SRCs. The only supervision of these institutions is by visiting Home Office officials and this is thought to be inadequate by many people. We have also received complaints from the relatives of inmates. At present visits are only allowed on the third Thursday of the month. We think there is some substance in the complaint that this is inadequate, although we appreciate the point made by administrators that visits tend to undermine the morale of the patients and hamper the work of the therapists, who claim the right to ban all visits from friends and relatives when the patient is at a crucial stage of the treatment.

241. Another grievance concerns visiting hours, which are 9am – 11am at SRCs. Relatives of patients complain that it is almost impossible to get to these institutions so early in the morning because all Sexual Retraining Centres are in remote areas inadequately served by public transport. The SRCs that were originally established in towns have had to be moved out into the country because some patients lost all control of themselves and their screams disturbed the residents living nearby. We suspect that these inconvenient visiting hours are part of the deliberate policy of the SRCs to discourage all contact between the patient and the community outside.

242. We have also heard some disturbing reports about the administration of discipline in SRCs. We understand that some

unruly patients have been given severe electric shocks, not as part of their course of treatment, but as punishment. We have also been told that obstreperous patients in HACs have been given extra large doses of steroids because this not only reduces their sexual drive, but also makes them quiescent and amenable. We are aware that this is no different from practices that were current in our mental hospitals long before the Sexual Containment Act was passed, but we are unhappy about the level of supervision in these institutions.

243. We think that a case has been made out for the formation of independent tribunals to deal with these grievances. The present procedure for dealing with complaints against the police is so obviously unsatisfactory that we hesitate to recommend a similar procedure. The leaders of the Union of Inspectors and Referendaries have told us, quite emphatically, that they are not prepared to accept any kind of tribunal. Anyone who gives evidence to a Government Committee can, of course, make categorical statements without the necessity of being impartial. Even so, we have not overlooked the fact that it would introduce a measure of discrimination if we recommended a really independent tribunal to deal with complaints against Inspectors and Referendaries, while policemen continue to judge the validity of most of the complaints made against the police.

## (h) SIFS's Evidence

244. We turn now to the evidence from SIFS. We have considered their views carefully and seriously, even though we would rather have been spared the demonstration of sexual techniques given to the Committee by their witnesses when we asked them to provide oral evidence; the sight was neither edifying nor instructive as far as this Committee is concerned, but the young are often ignorant about the knowledge of the old. We are determined that this miscalculation will not bias us against either their oral or written evidence.

245. SIFS is an amalgamation of several pressure groups which combined to form an organization whose main policy is 'to promote the individual's right to do his own sexual thing in his own private home.' In fact their subsequent statements have gone far beyond

this original intent. There has been a fair amount of internal dissention within the society. For example, when journalists ring up SIFS for information or comments, as often as not they are told that no one can come to the telephone because everybody is at a staff policy meeting. Quite recently their General Secretary was sacked because in the opinion of the Executive Committee he was 'sexist', but there was no general agreement among the members about this, or about the meaning of that word. But despite these occasional self-regarding wrangles, they are the only society that has diligently and consistently opposed the basic principles of the Sexual Containment Act.

246. The initials SIF stand for 'Sex Is Fun' and this probably sums up their philosophy very adequately. The acronym SIF is also intended to be ironic because syphilis ('syph' as it was called) was at one time the greatest threat to the enjoyment of sex; now it has been eliminated to all intents and purposes and no one need hesitate before he has sexual intercourse because of the fear of being infected by syphilis. SIFS maintains that it is time to explode all the other myths that stop people from enjoying sex.

247. The evidence from SIFS can be summarized simply by stating that they believe there is no universal moral code: It is both uncharitable and impertinent to impose one's own moral standards on others: Some people obtain great pleasure and satisfaction from sex and no one has the right to stop them, so long as their sexual activities do not harm anyone else: There are many more people who could get a great deal of fun from sex if only they were given help and encouragement instead of being deterred and restricted.

248. In an interesting addendum from a group of female homosexuals, it is argued that if, in their folly, the authorities feel it is essential to restrict sexual behaviour, the activity they should restrain is penetration, not orgasm; nearly all sex activities are harmless as well as delightful; the few that are harmful, such as rape, illegitimacy, abortion and most sexually transmitted diseases are the result of penetration, not of orgasm; restraints put upon orgasms attained through fantasy are particularly deplorable because these can be achieved only by means of a strong creative imagination, which is a precious gift to be encouraged and developed. These

views were also supported by the Campaign for Homosexual Equality, although not all male homosexuals are against all forms of penetration.

249. The evidence from SIFS is not really a criticism of the operation of the Act, but of the Act itself. In fact they are strongly opposed to the whole concept of sexual restraint. It is beyond the scope of this report to consider their central proposal that all sex is to be encouraged at all times and in all circumstances. Even so, we do not think their opinions are worthless and it would be a mistake to ignore their views. Consequently we are incorporating an extract from their written evidence in Appendix C and we urge readers to study this. Earlier we stated that one of the objects of this report was to promote public discussion. If this debate is to be meaningful, both sides of the argument should be heard.

## Exemptions

250. Who is to be exempt from wearing ORD? This has been the biggest problem the authorities have had to face. We are left with the impression that Ministers and officials did not give this question the earnest thought it demanded. They hoped it could be settled quietly with the minimum of fuss and were surprised by the discontent, jealousy and sheer bad feeling that this problem engendered.

251. It was originally announced during the second reading of the Sexual Control (Orgasms) Bill that the only exemptions would be Privy Councillors and a few other special cases. There were protests from the Women's Organization that 293 of the 300 Privy Councillors were men, but the main interest focussed on the so-called 'special cases'. Section 9 (8) of the Act permits the Secretary of State for Home Affairs to grant exemption to any person where there are 'special reasons why that person should not be subject to the obligations imposed by this Act.' The list of distinguished men and women who are specifically exempted has remained secret and the government has always insisted that the names on this list cannot be made a matter of public debate.

252. It is now known that the legal advisers of the Queen were in touch with the Home Office before the Act received the Royal Assent. An internal departmental memorandum (recently leaked by

the *Yorkshire Post* and so no longer on the secret list), headed 'ORD – THE QUEEN'S PRIVACY', suggested that the most tactful way of dealing with the matter would be to make *all* Heads of State exempt. Eventually the government decided that four classes of people would be automatically exempted in addition to those specifically named by the Home Secretary. These four classes were: Privy Councillors, members of the Cabinet, foreign ambassadors and all Heads of State. Other members of the Royal Family felt they were eligible because they often act as the representative of the Head of State; this point was conceded and they were exempted, but because one or two of them do not set the best possible example, they were required to give an undertaking that they would only have sexual intercourse with subjects who were bona fide members of the aristocracy; they were, of course, allowed to have sexual relations with the direct descendants of foreign royalty.

253. This is more or less the situation today. The list of exempted persons remains a secret and no one knows who is on it until they take their clothes off.

254. We have received various suggestions from our witnesses about people who should be exempt. The most popular suggestion is that there should be a system of special awards for service to the community. In fact we are able to reveal for the first time that such an arrangement is already in existence. A list of possible candidates is kept up to date by a patronage secretary attached to the Prime Minister's office. From time to time people who have rendered distinguished service to the community are sent a letter, ostensibly from the Queen, asking if they wish to receive a Merit Exemption (ME). It is an essential condition that they keep their ME absolutely secret. If they allow it to become known that they have been granted a ME, the entitlement is withdrawn and they are refitted with ORD.

255. Merit Exemptions are given to people in all walks of life but mainly to those who are prominent in public affairs. A person who has made a large financial contribution to a political party is quite likely to receive the ME when that party is in power. In some ways it works like the Honours System, except that the ME is far more highly prized than the CBE or OBE. When a senior Cabinet Minister lost his seat at the last general election, there was some

surprise when he did not become a Life Peer, but it is rumoured that he preferred the ME to the House of Lords.

256. The secret has been well maintained. This is probably because it is based on a formula that has been used in the National Health Service for many years. This is the system of covertly granting special financial awards to senior consultants. Just as it is possible for consultants to be working together in a hospital without knowing who is receiving a merit award, so it is possible for colleagues to be working together in a political or business organization without knowing who has been granted the ME. There have been occasions when a girl has been flattered by a distinguished man who offers to spend one of his orgasms with her, only to discover that he is exempt and the sole limit to the affair is the extent to which her own quota is expendable. On rare occasions a couple go to bed together and discover they both have the ME; then the only limit is age and fatigue.

257. It has been suggested to us that eugenics should be given greater weight. The National Flag, for example, believe that people who can prove that they come from a long line of pure British stock should be encouraged to breed unhindered by ORD. People with high IQs have also been suggested as candidates for exemption. Another suggestion combined aesthetic and eugenic factors; for genetic reasons dark hair tends to dominate fair hair, and brown eyes dominate blue; so when two blue-eyed blondes decide to mate, they should be exempt at least until they have produced four blue-eyed fair-haired children.

258. Other suggestions for exemption were Dowager Duchesses, Archbishops, athletes competing at international meetings (the extra weight of ORD was thought to be an unfair handicap in events like the high jump), deprived and under-privileged families (because they cannot afford any other pleasures), and Roman Catholic priests (a rather frivolous suggestion from the choir boys at Liverpool Cathedral).

259. We do not have an answer to this intractable problem. It might have been better if the government had decided that there should be no exceptions at all, but clearly this is no longer practicable. There may be something to be said for being less secretive about it. On the other hand, it is feared that if the award of each

ME were given publicity in the press, the political party in power might be tempted to curry favour by granting thousands of them in the weeks before a general election. There is also the possibility that the recipient of a publicly awarded ME may not be able to cope with all the offers that come to hand.

260. We believe the problem of exemptions is a threat which the government must take very seriously. The public will continue to accept the idea of sexual containment as long as they feel that it is the same for everyone (– or nearly everyone, because most people would agree that there should be a few exceptions, like the Queen, for example). The main cause for resentment is the feeling that some people are managing to do better out of it than they are. That is why people can be so nasty when the klaxon sounds, and why exemptions can become a red hot issue if they are not dealt with tactfully.

261. The British people will put up with a surprising amount of inconvenience and will accept compulsory restrictions provided they apply to everyone. If the hardships are shared equally, not many people will complain or ask if the restraints are really necessary.

## Public Attitudes

### (a) The Survey Results

262. The Committee commissioned the Office of Population Censuses and Surveys to carry out a research on a representative sample of the population to get their opinions about the Act and their views on the permitted number of orgasms.

263. When the respondents were asked if they approved of the Sexual Containment Act, 47 per cent said 'Yes,' 20 per cent said 'No' and 33 per cent were categorized as 'Don't Know'. Although most people appeared to be reasonably content with the existing situation, it is remarkable how many people were undecided. An even greater number of people were unable to give a definite answer when they were asked if they approved of the present level of the PNO; 17 per cent were satisfied, 28 per cent were dissatisfied and over half (55 per cent) could not make up their minds one way or the other. These results suggest that most people do not really have very strong opinions about sexual containment.

264. Towards the end of each interview when the confidence of
the respondent had been gained, it was possible to ask questions
about activities as well as attitudes. The respondent was asked if he
(or she) had used the full quota of orgasms in the last complete 13
week period. Over half (54 per cent) had done so and 4 per cent
were unsure, but 42 per cent replied that they had not used the
full number of permitted orgasms. These replies came from the
whole sample, which included a number of respondents who were
single, divorced or widowed, and this helps to explain the large
number who had less than the PNO in the last quarter. Taking only
those who were married, it was found that 28 per cent had not
experienced the maximum number of permitted orgasms (67 per
cent had done so and 5 per cent didn't know).

265. The answers to these four questions are set out in tabular
form on the facing page. The government can feel gratified by the
number who approve of the Act, but should take heed of the large
number who have not made up their minds. One third of the population do not at this moment in time seem to be very concerned, but
if for one reason or another a well organized campaign should increase discontent, then eventually the opponents of this Act would
be in a majority. On the other hand, history tells us that the longer
an Act has been in force the more people come to accept it without
question; it therefore seems probable that many of those who are
unsure about this legislation at present will feel less and less inclined
to oppose it as they grow older. It may not be many years before
moral spokesmen look upon the Sexual Containment Act as a
corner-stone of the British Way of Life.

266. It is not really surprising that some respondents, and men
in particular, should say that the PNO is not high enough, but this
may be bravado. At all events, a significantly large number of
respondents, including a quarter of the married men and women,
did not have the maximum number of permitted orgasms in the 13
week period before the interview.

267. All respondents who were over twenty-one when the Act
was passed were asked if they now have sexual intercourse more
or less often than before they were fitted with ORD. Nearly half
(47 per cent) said they had sexual intercourse less often than
before, but 30 per cent said that it had made little difference and a

**Attitudes to the Sexual Containment Act**

| Question | Yes % | No % | DK % |
|---|---|---|---|
| Do you approve of the Sexual Containment Act? | 47 | 20 | 33 |
| Do you approve of the PNO being set at its present level? | 17 | 28 | 55 |
| Did you use your full PNO quota in the last 13 week period (all persons)? | 54 | 42 | 4 |
| Did you use your full PNO quota in the last 13 week period (married persons only)? | 67 | 28 | 5 |

*The replies in percentages to four questions put to a sample of 2,000 men and 2,000 women stratified by socio-economic status so as to be representative of the population of the United Kingdom.*

surprising 23 per cent said they had sexual intercourse more often since the inception of ORD. These figures include some people who were single when the Act was passed and have since got married, but even among those who were married before they started to wear ORD, 15 per cent say they now have sexual intercourse more often. Furthermore over a half of those married respondents who said they did not use up their full PNO quota (in answer to the fourth question in the table) now have sex more often than they did before. So it seems reasonable to conclude that some married couples look upon the PNO as a kind of norm. Previously they may have felt unsure of themselves and been anxious not to appear abnormal by demanding too much sex from their married partners. Now they have a standard on which they can base their own sexual activities and if, as in some cases, this is rather higher than what they had been used to, they valiantly strive to keep up to standard.

268. When this research is compared with earlier surveys[30], the

---

[30] Schofield, Michael, *The Sexual Behaviour of Young Adults*, Allen Lane, 1973. Gorer, Geoffrey, *Sex and Marriage in England Today*, Nelson, 1971.

results confirm that the Act has had a levelling effect. Those who had high sexual frequencies are now legally prohibited from having as much as they once had, and those who had low frequencies tend to come up to the permitted maximum. These survey results also suggest that the impression of universally high sexual frequencies prior to the Act (as reported by our officials in Part I of this report) may have been misleading.

269. According to SIFS the Act puts a burdensome obligation on those who prefer low frequencies and has a deleterious effect on those who need high frequencies. We have seen no conclusive proof that sexual limitations cause physical damage. There is some evidence that sexual limitations increase the general level of tension and testiness, but we have seen no conclusive proof that they cause permanent psychological distress. The Categorical Society always assumes that those who do not use their full quota are more contented than the others, but we are not yet convinced that happiness is the inevitable by-product of sexual restraint.

## (b) The Act Is Accepted

270. If they had been asked whether the public would stand for such a radical change as the Sexual Containment Act, even as little as five years ago, most people would have said that it was out of the question. And yet three years after the Act has been in operation, less than a quarter (20 per cent) oppose it and only a few more (28 per cent) disapprove of the present level of the PNO. This is a most remarkable change in attitudes and it is important that we try to understand why this has happened.

271. We suggest there are three main reasons. The first one was noted in the previous section when we were discussing exemptions. The public will put up with all sorts of impositions as long as they feel that everyone else is having to carry the same burden. It used to be called 'the Dunkirk spirit' during the Second World War. Rationing was accepted with a smile; anger was reserved for those who traded on the black market or for the few famous people who went off to America.

272. The results of our commissioned survey indicate that most people will accept restrictions and many of them positively want

to feel that their sexual activities are similar to everyone else's. Another question in the survey is also relevant here. Respondents were asked if they felt that some people were managing to evade the regulations; most people (67 per cent) thought not, but there is an element of doubt in the minds of some people (14 per cent) and almost one in five (19 per cent) think there is some evasion. Our interpretation of these survey results is that, in general, the government has been successful in allaying the fears of the public, but there is nevertheless a small group of dissidents which will become larger if the exemption issue is not handled more tactfully and more scrupulously.

273. We have also hinted at the second reason why the Sexual Containment Act has been accepted by most people without protest. The demand for sexual intercourse before the inception of ORD was not as strong as many had assumed (including the Home Office officials, who wrote Part I of this report) and this is confirmed by the results of the survey. It was always said that the fifteen years or so before the Act (1966–81) was the period of permissive sex, but looking back at it now, we can see that this is a long way from the truth. What made it seem so permissive at first sight were the commercial excesses of sex – the blue films, the porno shops, the strip clubs, etc. The demand for sex education, which should have been taught in the schools, was filled by publishers, film makers and others who regarded sex as a marketable commodity.

274. In those years reliable contraceptives were not readily available; abortions on the NHS were difficult to get; VD was still unmentionable; and sex education was woefully inadequate. There was a small minority who were very permissive, but for most people, sex was neither very plentiful, nor very enjoyable. The reason why it was not very enjoyable was:

(1) partly because the over-exposure of commercial sex contaminated private sex, making it all seem rather sordid, coarse and vulgar;

(2) partly because people were not much good at it.

As sex was not really the exciting sensuous pleasure it was made out to be, it was not too much of an imposition to be told you could not do it so often.

275. No one had bothered to explain to the on-coming generations that sexual pleasure, like most forms of enjoyment, is not something that one attains without some effort, but requires education and practice. Consequently, when the instant pleasures promised by the marketeers were not immediately forthcoming, many young people became disillusioned with sex. It is one of the axioms of marketing that repeat orders depend upon continuous demand. The early demand for sexual relations among the very young was certainly stimulated, but for many of them the much-vaunted pleasures of sex seemed to be unobtainable and the demand became less intense. So when the average person was first fitted with ORD, he (or she) may have occasionally felt frustrated, but the mood soon passed.

276. The third reason why the Act was accepted is that the organized opposition was very ineffective. It was expected that the left wing groups would provide the main opposition. George Orwell thought he saw 'a direct intimate connexion between chastity and political orthodoxy.' But the militancy of the left was (as ever) dissipated by internecine strife. It used to be said that nothing would provoke a pacifist group to violence except the sight of a rival pacifist group. Similarly, no argument between a Conservative and a Socialist can engender the same level of bitterness as a discussion between two revolutionary Marxists. But rhetoric butters no parsnips and neither the government nor the public were much impressed by the opposition to the Act that came from the left wing movement. SIFS was not a very effective organization in those early days, even though latterly it has provided the main opposition to the Act. We have already said that we consider their evidence useful, but we also think they have missed the main objection to the Act by concentrating on the sexual aspects. Too many of the points they make are below the belt, for it is not the restraints put upon exercising the genitals that is the concern of this Committee, but the restrictions on the individual's rights and liberties.

## (c) A Warning and the Conclusion

277. There is no direct evidence to support the SIFS conclusion that the Sexual Containment Act is harming the economic or cultural life of the community. People who want to exceed their

PNOs do not appear to be especially gifted or superior in any way. Are those who are over-sexed better artists, better musicians, better businessmen, better civil servants? An analysis of those who have been sent to HACs or SRCs provides no evidence which would support this view. We are bound to agree with those who claim that it is impossible to show that the Act is doing any serious physical harm by restricting their sexual activities.

278. But there is one fundamental objection to this Act. No matter what the benefits may be, there is an area of human activity which is absolutely private and not the concern of the state. Within that area a few citizens may do things which are indirectly detrimental to the welfare of the state; many more will do things which are unproductive, unusual or just plain stupid. This is their right. The benefits of state interference within that small area cannot compensate for the serious loss of individual liberty when this right to privacy is taken away.

279. Some of us on the Committee are unhappy about the existing situation and are far from convinced that the advantages of the Sexual Containment Act outweigh the disadvantages. But all of us agree that the Act cannot now be repealed. The public have grown to accept it and comprehensive changes would be too disruptive in the present circumstances.

280. But if we cannot go back, at least we can take a warning for the future. We must be more vigilant when we have to balance social benefits against individual rights. For example, it has been suggested that the problems of over-population can be solved by compulsorily limiting each family to two children.[31] Another suggestion is that homes should be wired so that all private conversations could be recorded; technically this would be quite easy to do and would be of benefit to the community because the tapes could be checked, not only in security cases, but also for divorce proceedings, conspiracy charges, credit rating and to catch viewers who have not bought a TV licence. But the overwhelming argu-

---

[31] One demographer has suggested that a fairer arrangement would be to put families into groups of ten and allow them to have as many offspring as they liked so long as the average per family did not exceed 2·3 children. When the maximum had been reached all further pregnancies would be terminated.

ment against such suggestions is that they would be an impertinent intrusion into our private lives. A similar argument could have been used against ORD when it was first being tried out.

281. The government's answer to the Committee's concern is that the price of high moral standards is bound to be the limitation of personal freedom. They argue that there are ample precedents for state interference into the sex lives of British subjects. For example, the cohabitation rule administered by the Supplementary Benefits Commission encourages investigating officers to question the neighbours, relatives, employers and landlords of women claiming benefit to ask if they are entertaining men friends.

282. But we wonder if it is really the sexual aspects of the situation that are relevant. We suspect that sexual containment may be the means by which all new ideas and constructive criticisms are rejected. The social health of the community depends upon the conflict between youthful activists and the defenders of the status quo. Sex is the area of human activity where the new ideas of the young are most likely to be in conflict with the traditional ways of the old. We must be sure that our urgent desire to restrain sexual behaviour is not confused with our general alarm at the way the old social and political orthodoxies are being challenged.

283. We raise these matters in this report because we hope it will provoke public discussion. We fear that the continuing economic crisis has narrowed people's interest so that their concern with the cost of living and the size of the wage packet has diminished their interest in wider issues. If you are not interested in public political events, you don't have to worry about them. But if people do not stand up for their civil liberties, then they will lose them, one by one, until even the freedom to protest will be lost.

284. Already people are beginning to forget what it was like in the old days when sex was not restricted. When freedom is forgotten, perhaps it will not be missed. Is happiness the facility to forget inconvenient facts?

285. Although this report is about sexual containment, the concern of this Committee is not about sex. It is about apathy. We have come to the sad conclusion that people would prefer to be

ordered not to do something than told to take action. They want stability and this requires a solid system of hard and fast rules. Life is simpler, quieter, cooler, when the possibilities are limited.

PART IV

# RECOMMENDATIONS

286. Although we are not entirely satisfied with the existing situation, it is fair to say that the Sexual Containment Act is operating reasonably efficiently. We believe that there is insufficient unanimity among the public for us to recommend fundamental changes. In particular, our main concern (summarized in the final paragraphs of Part III) is not shared by the general public. Accordingly we have decided to make no recommendations.

APPENDIX A

# TECHNICAL AND ANATOMICAL PROBLEMS

## Brief Resumé of Possible Male Recording Devices

It has long been observed that the clearest sign of sexual excitement in the male is the erection of the penis. The study of the anatomy and physiology of penile erection has been exhaustive and as the increase in size is normally very pronounced, it would seem at first glance to be the best method of measuring sexual stimulation. However, there are several disadvantages:

It should not be presumed that every incidence of increased vasocongestion or of muscle tension observed in the male penis necessarily reflects a state of sexual excitement. It is well known that men and boys frequently suffer from firm erections when they wake up in the morning. Recurrent penile erections have been recorded during experimental studies of male subjects while they have been asleep. In younger males erections during dreams have often been observed despite ejaculatory experience in the immediate pre-sleep period. Involuntary penile erection is also found in certain pathological conditions, such as phimosis where the foreskin is so tight that it cannot be drawn back over the glans and the entrapped smegma causes proprioceptive stimulation. The penis can also become erect in situations which are not apparently sexual, such as riding on a bus, lifting heavy loads, or straining on the lavatory. A further complication is that penile erections have been observed in very young boys. The causes of an erect penis are so variable that it cannot be used satisfactorily as a measure of individual sexual response.

These difficulties are even more intricate when attempts are made to measure increases in the size of the clitoris as sexual excitement develops. Accordingly most researchers decided that the best method of estimating the extent of sexual excitement in both the male and female would be a device that would measure the number of orgasms.

The main feature of the male orgasm is ejaculation and this presented certain difficulties. Although many designs were tried out on volunteers from the prison population, all the instruments had to be clamped on the end of the penis and inevitably this caused a certain amount of discomfort during sexual intercourse. Doctor Waxman's ingenious design, which resembled an extension of the penis, was popular with some men who were not well endowed, but the technical problems proved to be unsurmountable. No doubt the rough edges reported by the female volunteers could have been eliminated by improvements in the manufacturing process, but the problems of hygiene and infection were never solved.

Many research workers concentrated on the contractions of the sphincter urethra, bulbospongiosus, ischiocavernosus and transverse superficial perineal muscles during orgasm. But after the first three or four major expulsions, the contractions are much less explosive and become irregular. These minor contractions which continue for several seconds make accurate measurement more difficult and the resulting record is often confused and difficult to read.

It was known that the testes increase in size and rise to a position close to the perineum during sexual stimulation. The difficulty is that this occurs at an early stage of sexual excitement and is not really an indication of orgasm. If sexual stimulation is continued and the man goes on to reach an orgasm, no further reaction of the testes will be recorded. Similarly the skin of the scrotum thickens at about the same time as the penis becomes erect, but there does not appear to be any further reaction of the scrotal sac just before or during orgasm. After many months of study, the workers at the government research institute were forced to turn away from the external genitalia of the male and look elsewhere.

## The Development of the Orgasm Recording Device

It had been known for some time that the urethra not only lengthens but increases in diameter as sexual excitement increases. The real breakthrough occurred when it was noticed that the urethral bulb increased to almost three times its size just before orgasm (see Figure 1). This distension is of such magnitude that it can be seen by direct observation without the need for colposcopic examination.

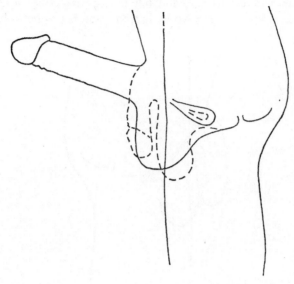

Figure 1

*The lateral view of the male genitals at the flaccid stage (dotted lines) and the orgasmic stage (unbroken lines). The urethral bulb increases to more than twice its normal size at the orgasmic stage.*

The important point about this rapid distension of the urethral bulb is that it is pathognomonic of impending orgasm;[1] in other words when the bulb has more than doubled its size, orgasm is certain to follow. It is believed that this is the most satisfactory part of the male anatomy on which to make accurate enumeration of orgasms. The enlargement of the urethral bulb is a well defined reaction, a constant occurrence and a sure indication of impending orgasm. It was not long before a neat instrument was devised to fit closely beneath the perineum (see Figure 2). This recorded every occasion when the urethral bulb increased by more than twice its original size. Although the dimensions of the urethral bulb do vary slightly from one man to another, it is impossible for a man to have

---

[1] It is the distension of the urethral bulb that helps the man to know when the ejaculation is coming according to Sherfey, M. J., 'The evolution and nature of female sexuality in relation to psychoanalytic theory', *J. of Amer. Psychoanal. Ass.,* (Winter issue), 1965.

an orgasm without the bulb doubling in size; conversely, if the bulb increases by more than twice its size, the man is certain to have an orgasm.

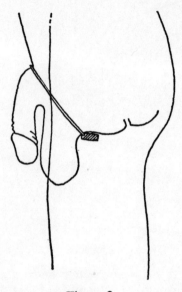

Figure 2

*Male genitals (lateral view) with ORD fitted.*

This orgasm recording device (or ORD as it came to be known) does not record every time a man gets an erection. Immediately after orgasm the distended urethral bulb shrinks quite a long time before the man loses his erection. Consequently ORD will record both orgasms when a man has two over a short period of time without losing his erection; young men who are capable of multiple orgasms will gain no special advantage because each ejaculation will be recorded by ORD.

This device is hygienic, easy to keep clean and, of course, waterproof. The male ORD is attached to the perineum by means of clips on the scrotum and by a swivel arm that is swung round to make a ring through which the penis and the testicles hang freely (see Figures 2 and 3). Protracted tests were carried out in government laboratories to find the optimum placement which would provide the minimum interference during sexual intercourse, inceptive activities, masturbation or nocturnal emissions. All orgasms are, of course, recorded no matter what method may be used.

The remaining details are more administrative than technical. The device is sealed after it has been fitted in order to discourage people from tampering with it. Unfortunately there have been a few cases of vandalism, sometimes by men exasperated by their inability to control their orgasms, but usually by crafty engineers who have tried to re-set the mechanism so that fewer orgasms would be

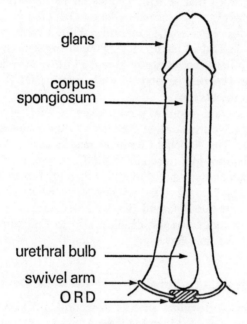

Figure 3

*The erect penis (ventral view) with ORD fitted.*

recorded. This necessitated modifications to the original specifications and ORD (Mark II) now incorporates a klaxon which is activated when the seal is broken. The klaxon continues to emit a high pitched sound until the vandal reports to the Inspectorate where, after paying a small fine, he is refitted with a new device.

Unfortunately there were some cases in the early models of ORD (Mark II) when the klaxon started to sound even though the seal had not been broken. This was the cause of much embarrassment, especially if the subject had to travel to the Inspectorate by public transport. It is believed that this fault has now been rectified.

ORD is of robust construction and very few mechanical or electronic faults have been reported. Of course one must discount those cases where the subject has enjoyed more than the permitted number of orgasms and complains that the recording mechanism must be faulty. There was one case in which a subject appeared to have had only 7 orgasms during the quarterly period, but subsequent enquiries revealed that he had experienced 107 orgasms during the previous 13 weeks. The original design of ORD did not allow space for a third digit because the authorities did not envisage the possibility of an individual having 100 or more orgasms in a 13 week period, but it has been necessary to make further modifications and now anyone who gets beyond 99 while wearing ORD (Mark III) will activate the klaxon.

Despite the good record of service given by ORD, it was decided for administrative reasons that each device should be checked every three months. The National Computer sends a card to each subject when it is time for him to report to the Inspectorate. The servicing takes less than an hour and during this time the record is taken out of the device and passed to the relevant Referendary who interviews the subject. All the Referendaries have had extensive training in counselling methods and this enables them to deal with any problems the subject may have.

## The Development of a Female Orgasm Recording Device

The problem of providing an orgasm recording device for women was even more complex than the difficulties encountered during the development of ORD for men. The neurophysiological parallel to penile erection in the male is the female's production of vaginal lubrication. But this is very variable and cannot be used as an objective measurement of sexual excitement.

The clitoris is the main sensory organ in the female and its primary function is to elevate sexual tensions, but there is marked variation in anatomical positioning, which makes it impossible to use this organ as a measuring device. Furthermore, a large number of women, perhaps a majority, do not develop clinically obvious tumescence of the clitoral glans and among those that do, the extent of swelling or elongation does not seem to correspond to the women's level of sexual response.

As the early work on the development of the male ORD shifted from measuring erections to enumerating orgasms, government administrators asked the scientists to use the same criterion for the female ORD. At first the researchers were doubtful about this because many believed that the female orgasm was often a psychological response to sexual stimulation. For example, it is often maintained that women can pretend to have an orgasm in order to please their partners. Women may be able to stimulate straining the muscles and contortions of the body, but the physiological reactions to orgasm cannot be imitated. These have been recognized and reported by many observers over twenty years ago.[2] The intensity of the sex flush is the most observable physiological reaction and there are others, such as high cardiac rates and elevated systolic pressures. The rapid detumescence of the areolae and the contractions in the outer third of the vagina remove any doubt as to whether a woman is pretending or really experiencing orgasm.

Both the basic anatomy and the physiology of the clitoris are too variable to be used to measure the number of orgasms, but there is one part of the female genitalia that would provide an excellent base for orgasmic enumeration. When a woman is sexually excited, the inner labia expand markedly in diameter and as she approaches orgasm they protrude through the outer labia.

Furthermore the inner labia produce a unique physiological reaction just before orgasm when they undergo a complete change of colour from pink to bright red (in nulliparous women) and to a deep wine colour (in multiparous women). The colour change is so obvious that it is called the 'sex skin' of the sexually stimulated woman. What made it particularly relevant for the scientists working on the development of the female ORD was the discovery that when a woman has produced this obvious change of colour in the sex skin, she is certain to experience an orgasm.

But despite the development of hyper-sensitive films which would record this change of colour in a camera located below (but not actually touching) the inner labia, it proved impossible to design

---

[2] Levine, L., 'A criterion for orgasm in the female', *Marriage Hygiene*, 1: 173–174, 1948. Hitschmann, E. and Bergler, E., 'Frigidity in women: Restatement and renewed experience', *Psychoanal. Rev.*, 36: 45–53, 1949. Hornstein, F. X. and Faller, A., 'Gesundes Geschlechts Leben', in *Handbuch fur Ehefragen*, Walter, 1950. Terman, L. M., 'Correlates of orgasm adequacy in a group of 556 wives', *J. Psychol.* 32: 115–172, 1951.

a device that would not be cumbersome and uncomfortable during sexual intercourse. It became obvious that the same difficulties would be experienced with any device that was fitted on or near the female genitals, so the scientists were obliged to seek other openings.

The first evidence of sexual excitement in the breasts is nipple erection, which is the result of involuntary contraction of muscular fibres within the structure of the nipple.[3] But the disadvantages of using this reaction as an enumerating device is that women with small nipples do not show a measurable increase in size. Furthermore the nipples often become erect at an early stage of sexual response and are not a sure sign of impending orgasm.

As sexual excitement increases there is a discernible enlargement in the size of the breasts. When the woman is standing, this effect can be seen in the lower part of the breast; when the woman is lying down the overall increase in size is still more apparent. This was first described by Dickinson over thirty years ago.[4] The unsuckled breast may increase to as much as one fourth of its original size (see Figure 4) but the breast that has been suckled does not

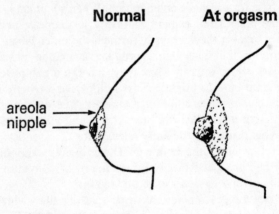

Figure 4

*The female breasts before sexual stimulation and at the orgasmic stage.*

[3] Gray, H., *Anatomy of the Human Body*, (43rd ed.), Lewis, 1982.
[4] Dickinson, R. L., *Atlas of Human Sex Anatomy*, (2nd ed.), Williams and Wilkins, 1949.

usually show such a definite increase in size. When more than one child has been suckled, the breasts rarely increase in size at all even after prolonged sexual stimulation. The change in breast-size is unsuitable as a measuring device because it does not always apply and also because the breasts swell early during the sexual response and (in the nonsuckled breast) maintain their enlarged size long after orgasm.

But there is one reaction of the breast that is far more suitable as a measurement of orgasm. When a woman is really excited, the areolae swell so that they impinge upon the nipples, creating the illusion that the sexually stimulated woman has partially lost her nipple erection (see Figure 4). At the same time the areolae become enlarged and engorged with blood, but it is the easily observed tumescence that can be measured with a special device. This swelling of the areolae occurs whether the woman has ever been pregnant or not, and whether her breasts have been suckled or not.

The special feature of this reaction is that the onset of orgasm is followed immediately by the detumescence of the areolae (see Figure 5). When this swelling dies down, the nipples appear to

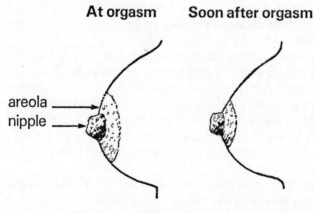

**At orgasm**       **Soon after orgasm**

areola

nipple

Figure 5

*The female breasts showing that the nipples are still erect soon after orgasm but the areola quickly returns to its normal size.*

gain full erection. This has been called the 'false erection' and some women are under the impression that it is a new phase of sexual excitement. In fact the nipples have been erect throughout the period of sexual stimulation and it is simply the early detumescence of the engorged areolae occurring long before the nipple erection subsides which produces this effect.

The swelling of the areolae is usually, but not always, a sign of impending orgasm in the female. But when a record of the swelling is immediately followed by a rapid detumescence of the areolae, then one can be certain that orgasm has occurred. This means that the orgasm recording device must include a small electrographic tracing so that both the swelling and the deflation can be recorded. When this record is taken out of ORD it can be fed into a reading machine which magnifies the tracing over 5,000 times and so the number of orgasms in the quarterly period can be counted by the Referendary in less than a minute.

The great advantage of using the areolae as the basis for recording female orgasms is that the occurrence is constant at all times, including all three trimesters of pregnancy and also after the woman has given birth. It also has the great advantage over any device that uses part of the genitals as a basis for recording in that it can be fitted without causing hindrance or discomfort during most sexual activities.

The small reactor fits round the nipple with a lead that runs to the ORD, which is attached to the muscular fibres under the breast (see Figure 6). As the ORD for the female has to incorporate a tracing record, it has to be a little larger than the male ORD, but this causes no inconvenience because the beautifully designed device fits neatly under the breast. It is not necessary for the woman to wear two ORDs because the areola under each breast react in consort.[5]

Some men have complained that the female ORD inhibits them during sexual foreplay, but few women have complained. A man tends to enjoy fondling his partner's breasts and is often disappointed when he discovers that this does not give the girl as much pleasure as it gives him.

---

[5] If the nipple had been used as an indication of impending orgasm, it would have been necessary to fit two because it frequently happens that one nipple may become erect while the other one remains quiescent.

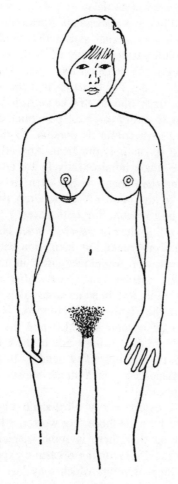

Figure 6

*The small reactor fits round the nipple and a lead connects it to the ORD under the right breast.*

The female can return to a state of orgasmic capability much more rapidly than the male, and she is able to maintain an orgasm for a relatively longer period of time. These two important differences in orgasmic expression were the cause of some concern to the authorities when ORD was first introduced.

Many males have learnt to delay ejaculation while their partner has several orgasms in quick succession. Furthermore, when women concentrate on their own sexual satisfaction 'without the psychic distractions of a coital partner'[6] many of them need three or more orgasms before they reach satiation and some would go on longer if it were not for lassitude. The question that the authorities had to ask themselves was this: Should this be regarded as one orgasmic experience or should every orgasm be counted? The decision was to make ORD as accurate as possible so that every orgasm can be recorded so far as it is practical. Any adjustment thought necessary could be made administratively by allowing women to have more orgasms than men. In the event it was decided (for reasons explained in the body of the report[7]) that the permitted maximum should be the same for both sexes.

It is worth reiterating that breast-size, inner labia coloration or nipple erection could not make the distinction between orgasms as accurately as the present techniques used in the female ORD. Detumescence of the areolae immediately after orgasm has been experienced is very rapid and in some cases takes place even before contractions within the vagina have stopped. This reaction is so quick that the areolae become wrinkled and the gradual rise and sudden fall depicted on the tracing made in the ORD is unmistakeable when viewed on the magnified reader. If orgasm does not occur, areolar detumescence is a much slower process and the wrinkles do not appear.

Thus ORD will detect nearly all female orgasms. The only exception seems to be with those few women whose orgasm lasts for such a long time that there is some suspicion they may be having a series of rapidly recurring orgasmic experiences. Subjects who report these long orgasms, which may last from 20 to more than 60 seconds, say that they are experiencing successive orgasmic peaks, but ORD does not record these and for administrative purposes they are regarded as one orgasm only.

In most other ways the female ORD is similar to the male version. It will record all orgasms however obtained, including those ex-

---

6 'Masturbating women concentrating only on their own sexual demands, without the psychic distractions of a coital partner, may enjoy many sequential orgasmic experiences . . .' page 65 of Masters, W. and Johnson, V., *Human Sexual Response*, Little Brown, 1966.
7 Paragraphs 210–213.

perienced during sexual intercourse, inceptive activities and masturbation with or without mechanical aids, such as vibrators or dildoes.

The wearer receives a card from the National Computer every three months so that she can bring in her ORD for servicing. While this is being done, a Referendary studies the tracings and makes a note of the number of orgasms. After counselling, the ORD is refitted. Most women's wear is now designed to incorporate ORD on the right breast and some designers have made a special feature of it, decorating the reactor with lace trimmings. Subjects, however, may elect to have it fitted on the left if they want a change.

Like its male counterpart, the female ORD has a good service record and very few faults have been recorded. Some confusion was caused by the enterprising firm that manufactured dummy female ORDs for male transvestites and there were genuine difficulties with the few hermaphrodites who reported to the Inspectorate, but otherwise it can be said with no little pride that the technical problems have been solved.

H

---

APPENDIX B

# CASE HISTORIES

## Introduction

The survey which we commissioned (see paragraph 3) was conducted on the basis that all the information given to the Committee would be treated as confidential. This Appendix consists of ten transcriptions from recordings taken at the interviews. These case histories have been added to our report because they refer to particular instances of exceptional relevance, given in the subject's own words, except for a few alterations made so that confidential material cannot be identified.

## Case History No. 1

*Mr G. A married man of 46, from Bristol*

'Mr H. (his Referendary) is a nice man, but I wish he wouldn't keep making jokes all the time. Last week was too much. He knows I'm a bit shy. I've always been a bit sensitive about sex and that. After I'd undressed he gave my balls a tap and said "Anyone for tennis?" Then when the time came to replace the ORD, he took a large metal tube and shoved it between my legs and said it was a new model. Then he laughed and said it was only his little joke. On another occasion I got a bit stiff. Well, you can't help it when someone's messing about down there and he started making remarks. He said I ought to be careful with a dangerous weapon like that and he went on about it nearly putting his eye out. I've thought of asking for a transfer, but I don't like to because he means well, really.'

## Case History No. 2

*Mr B. A shop assistant aged 19, from London*

'. . . Then one time I went over the limit, not much, only two in fact, but we went to Brighton for the Bank holiday week-end and we just went on and on, know what I mean. You don't think about it at the time, do you, but when the card came from the National Computer, I knew I'd had too many and you can imagine how I felt, I mean, I may look as if I don't care, but I do, you know, deep down inside. I've never been in no trouble before. Well, this Referendary could see I was shaking and he did his heavy bit and said it was a very serious matter and all that and I'd get a big fine if I didn't co-operate. And so I said I'd co-operate because I didn't really know what he was on about, and it turned out that what he wanted to do was suck me off. Honestly I didn't know what to say. I couldn't believe it. I thought he was trying to trap me or something. I mean, it's the last thing you'd expect from a Referendary. So, anyway, I let him, and when it was all over, he thanked me, would you believe. Then he said he'd see I was all right if I came to see him once a week, which I do every Wednesday afternoon 'cause it's early closing and in return he lets me have four extra PNOs, not counting the time I'm with him. It's been going on like this for almost a year now, so what with one thing and another, I'm getting 16 extra every quarter, no 17. Yes it must be 17 and that can't be bad, can it?' (Interviewer: 'Was that the first time you'd had oral-genital experience?') 'You've got to be joking.'

## Case History No. 3

*Ms W. A filing clerk of 24, from Wolverhampton*

'Before I was first fitted, I hated the idea, but once it was on, I soon got used to it and it didn't worry me much. Then I met this bloke, Jim and he said he'd been told of this fantastic trick of re-wiring ORD so that it didn't count the number of times I went with a fellow, type of thing. He reckoned he could do it without breaking the seal. This was before they fitted the buzzer.

Naturally I was a bit suspicious. I'm not stupid you know. I mean, it wasn't likely that an idiot like Jim would know how to do something that others would give a fortune for. Honestly, I can't think what came over me. We were drinking and carrying on, you know how it is, and then we went back to his place and I let him try to open the casing on my ORD. Just for a giggle, really. Jesus! He was a bit rough. It was hurting and I was bleeding and scream-ing for him to be careful. Then after a bit he said I had nothing to worry about 'cause he'd stopped it working. I didn't know if he had or he hadn't to be honest, but I had an idea he'd broken the seal, so I thought I was probably in for it when next I had to go and see the Inspector, so I let him do what he wanted.

When we'd finished, sort of thing, I got up and got dressed. On the way back – I only live three streets away – I happened to run into Henry, coming back from the pub. I've always rather fancied, Henry, so I said: "Hey, shall I tell you something that'll make you laugh?" At first he couldn't believe that my ORD wasn't working, but when he saw I meant it, well, Henry's not one to miss a chance like that and ten minutes later he was in my place in more sense than one, get my meaning, ha, ha!

After that, it just went on and on. Not with Henry, of course, because he couldn't afford no more because he's going out with that Sheila, but there were lots of others. You'd think, wouldn't you, with them all wearing ORDs, it would be hard to make use of my sudden freedom, but not a bit of it. There seems to be a lot of fellows around with one or two to spare. It was amazing. In fact when the word got round, I never seemed to stop. Even at work they'd come up to me and suggest we go to the storeroom. Actually, I didn't go to work very much that week. You won't believe it, but I must have had 40 or 45 men in ten days. It was ridiculous.

I don't know how long I could have gone on like that, but it all came to an end suddenly when the next caller was one of those Referendaries from the Inspectorate. Some sod must have reported me. I don't know for sure, but it was probably that Cyril. He's a mean bugger. No one likes him much, so he's usually got some to spare. He kept on pestering me, but when you're getting as many chances as I was, you can afford to be a bit fussy, can't you? So I told Cyril to get lost. Anyway this Referendary came to see me and I told him what had happened and we had a bit of a laugh about it and he sort of let me know that he might as well have a go as well before he took me back to the Inspectorate to have a new one fitted.'

## Case History No. 4

*Ms S. A 20 year old student, from Southampton*

'. . . After all the bragging and jokes about how the evening was going to end, Paul went very quiet when at last we were in the bedroom, just the two of us. He seemed to be rather shy. I thought, is this really the well-known stud the girls are always talking about? I started to take his clothes off and I felt that he'd got a hard on – with some relief, I may say. He'd been so quiet. He hadn't even kissed me and I must admit it crossed my mind that he might be gay. It wouldn't have been the first time that I'd discovered a he-man who was so in love with his own body, he couldn't get interested in girls.

He put out his arms and drew me close and soon most of that shyness and restraint had disappeared. He kissed me all over very slowly working his way down my body. It was marvellous, but we were still standing there in the middle of the room, so I took his hand and led him over to the bed. We lay there close – very, very close – and then after a time, after a lovely long time, he quietly and gently guided his prick and plunged into me, slowly at first, then quicker and longer, again and again. He squeezed my thighs in his grasp at every thrust he gave and kissed my neck and my lips. He was wildly passionate and yet so gentle, an incredible mixture of tenderness and tension.

At last I felt myself coming and I melted with a groan which filled the room. When he heard me, he let himself go with long contented sighs. We sank into a deep, dreamy, semi-conscious state and it seemed as if we would never move away from each other.

Then suddenly my klaxon went off. I jumped a foot and Paul, already alarmed by the piercing sound, got his prick wrenched as I jumped away from him. 'What shall we do?', I shouted. I don't think he heard me above the din. His face was white. We started to get dressed, but he couldn't find his underpants. I'd kicked them under the chair by mistake. Then the landlady started banging on the door. She wanted to throw a bucket of cold water over me, but by this time I was half dressed.

As for Paul, an hour ago the randy superman, half an hour ago the beautiful lover, now the shaking jelly. He sat on the bed with his head in his hands. I can't tell you the trouble I had getting to the Inspectorate. I can't bear to think of it, even now. Paul wouldn't come with me, the rotten bastard. He pushed a £5 note in my hand and said: "I must go now. I'm sorry. Good luck."

When it was all over and the Inspector had switched the bloody thing off, I asked him how it had happened. He said we must have been too rough. He said he'd had a couple in last week that got so excited that the bed collapsed and the girl, while trying to steady herself as she fell, grabbed hold of his cock and set off his horn. But I swear to you, it was just about the nicest, quietest sex I've ever had. Heaven knows I've been to bed with men who seem to think they've got some kind of battering ram between their legs, but not Paul. He turned out to be a nasty little coward, but he was a beautiful lover – gentle and skilful.

I'll tell you what really annoys me. I kept repeating to the Inspector that we were hardly moving when the klaxon started to sound, and he did admit that sometimes they did go off for no apparent reason at all. That's marvellous, I must say. You can imagine what this experience has done to my sex life. For a long time I wouldn't go with anyone. In fact I didn't go to bed with anyone until I met Ray. We're living together now and we'll probably get married and the sex is usually alright, but sometimes when we're making love, I suddenly freeze because I think I've heard that bloody klaxon and of course this upsets him as well. If I ever met the person who invented that thing, I'd murder him, honestly I would. I think it's absolutely scandalous that innocent people should have to put up with this. I feel so strongly about it and yet utterly helpless. No one will listen. No one believes you weren't tampering with the wretched thing. I get blazing mad when ever I think about it.'

## Case History No. 5

*Mr L. A man of 37 who works as a carpenter for the local council*

'I was talking to this chap in the pub. He seemed quite a sensible sort of a bloke and he was telling me that if you put your balls and prick in boiling water, it stopped the klaxon from working. I said, "But doesn't it hurt to put your balls in boiling water?" and he said, "Yes, it does a bit, but it's worth it because once you've made the klaxon unserviceable, you can open up the ORD and disconnect it." I didn't think too much about it at the time, but I mentioned it to my wife who was quite keen on the idea and went on about how nice it would be if I could stop my ORD working so that we didn't have to keep count. She kept on about how she always had to go short of it for the last weeks of the quarter because I'd been having a wank while at work and all that.

So we thought we'd try it. I didn't actually use boiling water, but I sort of hung them in a bucket with the water as warm as I could stand and then when I'd got used to that the wife put in some more from the kettle until really it was bloody hot by the time I'd finished. Then I took a screwdriver and slowly started to lever the cover off. But it's difficult to see what you're doing down there, and my hand slipped and it started, the fucking klaxon. I'd no idea it was so bloody loud. Christmas!

It was past eight at night when it happened, so the wife looked up the number of the local Inspectorate in the phone book, to see if it was still open. It's not under I you know. It's under bloody H, for Home Office Inspectorate. When she got through, it was one of those ansafone machines that said the nearest one was in Warren Street. So I thought, how the hell am I going to get there with this thing making this fucking noise?

It was too far to walk and I couldn't afford a taxi. I hadn't the money in the house. We were a bit skint, it being a Thursday and she'd been to bingo on the Tuesday. So there was nothing for it but the tube. I told the wife not to come and I ran to the station.

It was terrible, everyone looking and laughing and shouting. Then waiting for the bloody train. It was diabolical. All those remarks, like calling me "Dirty beast" and "Serve you right, you sex maniac." Some of them were just kidding like the chap who said, "What you been doing then? Riding your bike?" But I wasn't in the mood for jokes and anyway most of it was very nasty. One woman just came up and spat at me.

Then at last the train came in and I got in a carriage near the front. At first it wasn't very full but at the next station some yobos came in and they really set into me. One of them said, "Let's have him off; it can't do any harm now." Then two of them held my arms back and the others took my trousers down and started to wank me. Two of them were girls, you know. I swore at them, but they said, "I don't know what you're complaining about. You obviously like it so much you can't get enough of it." No one comes to your help. There were a lot of men and women there, pretending to look the other way, all prissy-like, but you could see them sort of stealing glances. I wouldn't be surprised if they weren't really enjoying it, the dirty buggars.

In the end I forced my way off the train at Euston, the station before Warren Street. I did up my flies and went up to the street and walked the rest of the way. It's easier on the street than the train. You can run away when people get too nasty. I got to the Inspectorate and would you believe it, it was fucking-well closed. I pressed the bell and a woman answered the door. She said it didn't open until midnight, and I said, could I come in anyway, and she said, it's only ten to nine, and I said, let me in anyway, but she said, no she couldn't do that. "I'm only the cleaner," she said. "There's no one else here. You'll have to go to Abbey Road. It says there on the door. Go to Abbey Road when this one's closed." And she shut the door.

By this time I was really pissed off, I can tell you. I don't know how long those batteries are supposed to last, but the klaxon was sounding just as loud as ever. Just then a taxi drove up and the driver leaned out and said, "I'll take you to Abbey Road for ten pounds." And I said, "Get off, it's only about two quid to Abbey Road." But he said, "Do you want a taxi or not? Right. It'll cost you ten pounds." So I told him I didn't have ten pounds and he said, "Have you got a watch? Let's have a look at it. Right, I'll take this instead. Get in." And so he took me there. I'd have given him anything by this time. I think he knew that. They say there are always taxis waiting around these places after they're closed and they'll only take people whose klaxons have gone off – at a price, of course.

When I got to the Emergency Inspector there were only two people in front of me; both of them had their buzzers sounding. There was a real old racket in that waiting room, I can tell you. The Inspector on duty was quite nice about it. He said it was bad luck and he didn't seem to want to know how it had happened. All he really wanted to know was how I was going to pay the fine. He wasn't really worried when I told him I was in a regular job. He said he'd arrange for £5 to be stopped out of my wages every week.

The strange thing is that I'd quite a few left before I'd have got to the end of my PNO, so why did I want to mess about trying to open the ORD? I don't know. It's like trying to get something for nothing, I suppose.'

## Case History No. 6

*Mr H. An executive aged 27, who works in an advertising agency in London*

'It all started so innocently during a discussion with this girl, Jane. We were both going to night school to learn Spanish and after the classes we usually had a snack at the café round the corner from the school. I didn't know Jane all that well, but she was good fun and I enjoyed chatting to her twice a week for about an hour before I caught the tube home. One night we got on to the subject of rape. I forget why. I think there'd been a report in the paper that day. Anyway, I said I thought it was impossible for a girl to be raped without her co-operating at least to a certain extent. I hadn't really thought this through very carefully, to tell the truth. For me it was just an academic discussion. What I didn't know was that Jane had been attacked by some nutcase who had raped her, or tried to. I didn't know this at the time, but I did notice that she was getting rather angry with me, which was unusual for her. I remember her saying rather bitterly that men had no idea of the sort of problems a woman had to contend with.

The following week she was quite friendly again and when we were in the café she suggested that we might go to Knebworth on the following Sunday where there was a special exhibition of jade. She knew I was particularly interested in Chinese art. I agreed to go, although to be honest I wasn't all that keen. I didn't want to become too involved with Jane. She was a bit too bossy for my liking. I prefer my girl friends to be more relaxed, more feminine, like my present girl Maria – I wasn't learning Spanish for nothing, you know. But I must admit that I was quite flattered that Jane was interested in me and it seemed to require no effort on my part. We'd go in her car and she'd bring along some sandwiches. All I had to do was provide a bottle of wine.

That Sunday we drove up the A1 and went round the exhibition and I honestly can't remember anything about it now. Then we had our sandwiches on the grass and had quite a lot to drink because Jane had also brought a bottle. Then we drove to Wheat-hampstead where we met two other girls who joined us in the car. Liz, one of the girls, suggested we find a secluded spot somewhere so that we could sunbathe. It was a warm sunny day and we found a field down some country lane and we all stripped off to bask in the sun.

The girls didn't seem to have any inhibitions about taking most of their clothes off, so when Jane suggested I take my trousers off, I didn't feel embarrased or anything. I lay there in my underpants in the warm sun, utterly relaxed, rather relieved that the arrival of Liz and the other girl, called Ricky, I think, had taken away the obligation for me to make a play for Jane.

Then after a bit of general chat, Jane brought up the subject of rape again and she told me about this madman who'd climbed through the window of her bedroom and attacked her. The others joined in the discussion and it became obvious that they had been told about my views by Jane. I just smiled when Liz asked me how I would resist if the roles were reversed and they had decided to rape me. Even when two of them held down my arms, I didn't put up much resistance. I still didn't suspect they had planned this together some days ago.

Suddenly the other two girls tightened their grip on me and Jane pulled off my underpants. I know this may sound exciting to some people. I've heard that some men fantasize about being seduced by a tough girl but, I promise you, this gave me no thrill at all. I was not excited, nor erect, nor enjoying it. If anything, I was embarrassed. I think my main reaction at that moment was fear of being seen by someone else – a farmer or a passer-by. I struggled, of course, but up to then I wasn't taking it very seriously. I thought they'd gone too far, but I was not at all prepared for what happened next.

They were quite strong and they slowly half-turned me on to my side, and then one of the girls, I'm not sure which one, put an instrument – Liz told me later it was her battery operated vibrator – up my arse. Of course, I realized then that this was no longer a joke and I swore at them and called them all the names under the sun and struggled like mad but I couldn't stop them.

I hadn't had anything to do with buggery since I'd left boarding school and I didn't expect to do it again or have it done to me, but when I felt this thing up me, it had a most powerful effect on me and – this is absolutely confidential, all this that I'm telling you, isn't it – well, I not only got a terrific hard on, but in a few moments I had a massive orgasm. When they saw I had come all over the place, the girls were as surprised as I was. Dismayed would be a better word. They did not intend to give me a sexual thrill. Far from it. Their intention was to degrade me and teach me a lesson by shoving this thing up my arse.

There's not much more to tell you. Eventually they took me to Harpenden and put me on a train. They'd wasted one of my orgasms, but that wasn't serious. I don't think I was using my full quota at that time. They taught me something about myself that I didn't want to know, but I don't think it had any lasting ill-effects. Except that I never did learn much Spanish. I couldn't face going back to night school and meeting Jane. For all I know, she may have felt the same about seeing me again, in which case her Spanish won't be any better than mine.'

## Case History No. 7

*Ms T. A 17 year-old unmarried typist, from Peterborough*

'I like wearing my ORD. Definitely. I wouldn't want to be without it. I'd feel sort of undressed without it. Of course, I would be undressed, wouldn't I, but you know what I mean. My friends say the same thing. I mean, it makes it alright, you know. I did have sex a few times without it, before I was 16, you know. I didn't like it much. Well, it seemed dirty, know what I mean. But ever since I've been fitted up, I don't mind at all. It will be different when I'm married, I suppose, but now a fellow chats you up and that, and after a bit he asks what number you've got to and if it's alright, I mean, not too much, he'll say, what are we waiting for then? I always like to find out about him as well. I mean, if he's right up near his PNO, then you know it will only be for the one evening, won't it? But if he's got a lot left, it probably means he's no good at it, doesn't it?'

## Case History No. 8

*Ms I. A radiographer aged 33, now working in Bradford*

'I went on this course when I was living in London with Roger. It's not the answer to everything, but it helps. It's also a rip-off, but I must admit that we had some laughs at the time. We made an appointment and paid in advance for the full course, cash down. They're very insistent about that, which is a shame really because some of those who paid their money didn't realize what they were in for and they gave up after a few sessions. Roger and I stuck it out to the end.

It's quite expensive and they pad out the course with a lot of blather – counselling, they call it. You know the sort of thing: "The male orgasmic process" and "the onset of ejaculatory inevitability". I remember all these quaint expressions because on the first day of the course the Principal gave us an inspirational lecture and then we were all presented with a red notebook and a ball-point pen, compliments of the college. The first part of the course – what you might call the O levels – is for men only and it consists of learning the squeeze technique. Basically – very basically – this means that one of the female staff starts to bring the client off, but then just before he comes, she squeezes the end of his prick and that stops him. After doing this a few times he begins to learn how to enjoy himself without having an orgasm. That's the theory, anyway. Roger said that some of the counsellors at the first session were really sexy girls and half the men had shot their load even before the girls had got their flies open, but at later sessions some old battle-axe did the squeezing and then she'd stand back and tell the pupil that his ejaculatory control was getting much better. That's an improvement?

That's about all there was to the first part of the course except they tried to sell you very expensive creams and jellies which were supposed to reduce "neurogenic end-organ sensitivity" – it says here in my notes. Roger says you have to be a bit careful because if you put the cream on the prick before it's stiff, it just lays there and sulks.

When they've learnt to control themselves, the men are encouraged to go and take their A levels, which they call "non-demanding intromission" and I call fucking without coming. Of course, for this part of the course you have to attend in pairs and each pupil brought along his wife, or girl friend or whatever. One man brought along his boy friend. If a pupil hadn't got a friend, the college would provide, at a large price, what they called "a replacement partner". A few weeks ago I wrote and asked them if I could have a job as a replacement partner, but they wrote back saying I'd have to take a special six-week course which would cost me £350, which is ridiculous.

Any road, Roger and I spent three afternoons a week learning "ejaculatory control orientation under proper therapeutic direction by retaining the penis intravaginally in a non-threatening environment" – you certainly learn all the jargon during the course even if you never learn to stop coming. In the lectures they kept talking about "mounting the female" which rather pleased Roger but made me feel like a bitch.

When you have managed to have sexual intercourse ten times without either of you coming, you've passed with flying colours. I've got my Diploma pinned up over my bed.

They always make out at the college that the second part of the course is essential. They blather away about mutual involvement and so on, but I'm told quite a lot of men have learnt to use the squeeze technique on themselves. I suppose that's OK as long as his wife or girl friend knows what he's doing. If he starts doing it with a strange girl, she's liable to fall out of bed laughing.

I've been told that there's a danger of the man becoming impotent if he takes this course, but I doubt it. Mind you, some of the men on our course were getting a bit limp towards the end, but I think that was just because they weren't used to having it off three times a week. It didn't seem to have any noticeable effect on Roger.

I don't know if there's a similar school where women can learn to have sex without coming. Roger says half the girls he fucks need lessons on how to *have* an orgasm and he's thinking of starting a school himself. I told him he'd started one years ago.

Then Roger and I split up and I came back to Bradford, and after a time I met this Bill who took a fancy to me, I could see that, but he kept putting me off. At first I thought, "Sod him, who needs him anyway". Then one day he told me his wife was very demanding and he simply could not afford to have an affair as well. Every one of his climaxes was ear-marked, so to speak. I told him not to worry and I explained about this system and how he could have good sex without coming off. He thought I was as daft as a brush, he really did. It took me ages to persuade him to try it, and when we did, it didn't work and he had an orgasm. I could see I really had a problem here, but I wasn't going to give up. Besides, now I wanted him because even after only one session I could tell he wasn't at all bad. He could teach even Roger a thing or two.

Well, there were one or two more occasions when I inadvertently deprived his wife of her prerogatives, the poor cow, but now we've got the hang of it. We don't do much fucking. It's mostly kissing and cuddling and mucking about. Then when I see he's right at the heights, I grab hold of his poor old John Thomas and I squeeze and I squeeze. He goes mad and pleads with me to let him come – he once offered me twenty quid – but I take no notice and keep right on squeezing. You can squeeze quite hard without doing any damage, or so they said at the college. In a short time – really just a few seconds – he's quietened down and then he's very grateful because we can start again and I've not lost him one of his precious orgasms. Then he can go back to his wife and have it off with her.

I think what they teach you at the college is quite useful if you can stick it out. On the course I was on, about a third of the pupils dropped out before the end. Of course the college wash their hands of them. They claim a high success rate and if it doesn't work on a pupil, they say he's got insufficient motivation. As I say, it is a bit of a racket, but there are some useful by-products. I noticed that communication between husbands and wives improved during the course. There seemed to be more understanding, more warmth. And, of course, it helped some to rid themselves of various fallacies and taboos. I must admit they helped me brush up my sexual techniques. Even Roger was rather pleased to find out about what they called "the lateral coital position".

I'd say that the squeeze technique works – for me, at any rate, if not for everyone. Mind you, I wouldn't recommend someone doing it for weeks on end without ever having an orgasm. But it's OK for Bill and me. He goes back to his wife and lets it all come out the same evening. Me? Oh, I can always abuse myself, as the saying goes. I think I prefer that, anyway.'

## Case History No. 9

*Mr C. A businessman aged 43, who lives in Surrey and works in Central London*

'I'd had this arrangement with the Inspector for some time. I didn't pay him much. Why should I? He didn't allow me much extra. Ten or twelve over the PNO, that's all. Anyway, I wasn't the only one giving him cash because all of a sudden the whole thing blew up and we had to appear at this investigation. It was a bit awkward really, because I didn't honestly know where I stood myself. It wasn't like a court of law. I wasn't allowed to bring my own solicitor and I didn't know how far I was liable to incriminate myself.

The man conducting the investigation was a Senior Inspector. He asked me a lot of questions and took a few notes, and then I heard that the whole enquiry had been postponed. I found out later that this Inspector, the one conducting the investigation, was being had up for bribery himself.

I don't know whether they were all in it together or what it was. I've been told that this man had two cars, one of them a Mercedes, and a house in Majorca. You can't do that on an Inspector's salary.

Of course, I'm guilty myself in a way. I was just paying out a few quid, buying myself a nice time, that's all. But these Inspectors, that's different. They were in it up to here. I don't agree with that sort of thing.'

### Case History No. 10

*Mr K. A storeman aged 32, who works in Peebles*

'I was seeing Diana, my girl friend, fairly regular and using up some of my NPO, or is it PNO, I never remember, and there wasn't always enough for Kate, that's the wife. Of course, I couldn't tell her about Diana; she'd have hit the roof.

So that I could have a good time with Diana every now and then, Kate had to do without, but she soon started to make a fuss about it and then one quarter I went over the maximum because I was desperately trying to please both of them. I paid the fine and managed to keep it quiet and I said to myself, "That's it. I'll have to give up seeing Diana." Though, to tell you the truth, I'd rather have given up having sex with Kate. Anyway, I didn't quite have the nerve to tell Diana that I wasn't coming to see her any more and of course the next thing that happens is that I'm over the number of permitted orgasms again. So this time I told the Inspector about these two women and the terrible trouble I was in.

Now it happened, though I didn't know it at the time, but there was this chap called McNab who'd been having trouble finding a decent girl, or so he said. The Inspector knew about it because this McNab always sort of apologized every time he came in because he had not used half his PNOs. So this stupid bastard – the Inspector, I mean – introduced McNab to my wife and more or less told them to get on with it. I suppose he thought he was doing me a favour, taking off the pressure, and it's true the wife did seem a wee bit more contented for a time. She wasn't always pestering me to come to bed early and things like that. And about twice a week I was fucking Diana – excuse my language – and everything seemed to be just working out perfect.

Then one evening I came home from work and I found the vacuum left in the middle of the living room and no dinner and a note from the wife to say she'd gone off with this fellow McNab. Well, of course I was very angry. Diana is quite good for an occasional fuck, but I could no' stand the thought of living with her. And anyway, Kate is my wife and I like living with her. So I managed to trace her through her mother and I ring her up and then the whole story comes out about her meeting McNab through this daft twit of an Inspector. Of course I've put in a complaint about him. You can't have an Inspector doing a thing like that. It's almost as bad as if he'd run off with my wife himself. So far I haven't had a reply from the Inspectorate. I've not heard from Kate either.'

I

APPENDIX C

# AN EXTRACT FROM THE WRITTEN EVIDENCE SUBMITTED BY SIFS (SEX IS FUN SOCIETY)

. . . It is nonsensical to think that there is one immutable moral code. Attitudes to sex vary according to regions, religion, backgrounds, sections of society and circumstances. With Haji 'Abdu' l-Yezdi we believe:

> There is no Good, there is no Bad;
> These be the whims of mortal will.
> What makes me weal, that call I good;
> What harms and hurts I hold as ill.
> They change with place, they shift with race;
> And, in the variest span of Time,
> Each Vice has worn a Virtue's crown,
> All Good was banned as Sin or Crime.

In this enlightened age we substitute 'normal and abnormal' for 'good and bad' and 'personality malfunction and social adjustment' for 'vice and virtue'. The sexually adventurous used to be called sinful; now we call them sick. But it is normal to be different because we all are in one way or another. What is appropriate sexual behaviour for one individual is unsuitable for another.

We reject the belief, unfortunately fostered by doctors as much as by churchmen, that there is one ideal direction for human sexuality. Even within one area and in one community there will always be a wide variation in sexual behaviour. Modern research, including the studies carried out by the Chairman of your Committee, does not support the idea that there is such a thing as 'natural' sex of a uniform sort. In his book on *Promiscuity* (published by Gollancz in 1976), Michael Schofield writes: 'My last research used a study group of less than 400 informants, all aged twenty-five, and yet there were some who had never had sex and some who started before they were sixteen; some had premarital intercourse and others were virgins when they married; some had only had one partner and some were promiscuous; some were exclusively homosexual, some were bisexual and some were exclusively heterosexual. It is unreasonable to expect uniformity, or seek to impose it, in such a personal matter.'

But now the legislators have taken this absurd idea of a uniform standard of behaviour one step further and have put restrictions on all sexual activities. This does not solve problems; it aggravates them. Sexual frustration leads to psychological and physical illness. When people are sexually satisfied, they feel better and work better. The Sexual Containment Act is depriving people of sexual satisfaction and so is harming the economic and cultural life of the community.

As long as there are moralistic laws like the Sexual Containment Act, there is the assumption that certain members of society have the right to control the sexual behaviour of others. Who gave them this right to use legal sanctions in order to enforce the morality of those who think they know best? We deny they have this right and we don't think they know best. This Act is a retrograde step, back into the past when the church had its own set of ecclesiastical laws which were enforced as rigorously as the civil law. We no longer have any use for moral guardians who claim the right to tell us what we should do and think.

It is always the older generation who have the power to make political decisions. This power is very likely to be abused when the decisions are about sexual activities. The less politicians have to do with sex the better, for laws are made by old people who have reactionary views on sex; they exaggerate the dangers and forget the pleasures.

Laws about sex are nearly always an extension of middle class morality. It is one social class telling another how they should behave. Not only is this high-handed, it is also hypocritical. It encourages the convention of two standards of morality – public pronouncements and private behaviour. The biographies of famous men frequently show that politicians publicly support standards of behaviour that they do not adhere to themselves.

Once you grant that the function of the law is to punish certain activities because one powerful group has decided that they are morally wrong or offensive, then any kind of sexual behaviour can be prohibited. At present the annual PNO is 108. Next year it could be 50. There are no limits on what restrictions can be imposed, once it is accepted that one group has the right to interfere in other people's sexual acts. This is just as oppressive when the power is wielded by an oligarchy of self-appointed moral guardians or by what John Stuart Mill called 'the tyranny of the majority'.

Even if it is accepted that certain members of a society have the right to control sexual behaviour, the standards laid down in the past almost certainly will not be appropriate to the conditions of today. This is particularly the case at the present time when ideas about what is sexually permissible are changing very rapidly. The new generations are right to question the old ethics and traditional moralities in the light of new discoveries such as more efficient contraceptives, safer abortion, new cures for VD.

The sex code cannot be changeless because many of the reasons for the prohibitions no longer apply. For example, the main reason for the ban on premarital sexual intercourse was to avoid illegitimate births which led to family feuds about the rights of succession. These considerations are no longer relevant.

New circumstances bring about new attitudes. Views about sex have changed quite dramatically. Not long ago church leaders and youth workers were implacably opposed to premarital sexual intercourse; now most of them accept it provided the couples are 'really in love'. Christians maintain that God's laws are immutable, but even a cursory examination of Christian teaching reveals fundamental changes in attitudes to sex. Fifty years ago the Pope was still insisting that sex not specifically for procreation was sinful, but now a married couple may 'with joyful and grateful spirit reciprocally enrich each other' – the Catholic way of saying it's now all right if you happen to enjoy sex.

Homosexuality was a terrible sin and the abominable crime. Now it is legal for consenting adults over 21. Headmasters no longer expel boys caught having sex together as long as it is thought to be no more than a passing phase; it is only a matter for concern if it looks as if a boy will have homosexual tendencies when he is grown up – which makes it difficult to explain why sex between boys is illegal but adult homosexual activities are legal.

For nearly 2,000 years there have been taboos forbidding conversation about sexual matters in most Western cultures. Even the simple anatomical details were thought to be immodest and distasteful. All that is in the past. As sex is now discussed quite openly, opinions will change even more rapidly than before, so it is quite ridiculous to expect everyone to abide by the same sexual standards for all time.

Not only will social attitudes change, but the circumstances for each individual will also change. We utterly reject the ludicrous assumption that a person's sexual needs are constant from 16 to 60. Most people will want periods of intensive activity followed by periods of diminished sexual interests. Those who want a lot of sex, those who want a little and those who do not want any at all should all feel assured of our understanding and support.

People have sexual intercourse for a variety of reasons; among others, because:

1. They love each other.
2. They want to have children.
3. They feel randy.
4. They want to find out more about each other.
5. They need reassuring about their own attractiveness.
6. They want to please the other person.
7. They enjoy each other's company.
8. They can't think of anything better to do.

All of these are private matters, the concern of two people and absolutely nothing to do with the government. Sex is a part of a person's innermost being. We strongly assert that private sex activities are not the concern of the law. As the Right Reverend John Robinson has said, where sexual behaviour is concerned, 'the function of the law in society is not to prohibit but to protect, not to enforce morals but to safeguard persons, their privacies and freedoms' (from *The Place of Law in the Field of Sex*, published by the Sexual Law Reform Society in 1973).

All the laws on sexual behaviour and particularly the Sexual Containment Act are muddled, full of anomalies, and in parts manifestly unjust. The sexual code consists of:

(1) Moralistic laws which say you must not do this because we, the lawmakers, do not approve of such behaviour.

(2) Paternalistic laws which say you must not do this because you may harm yourself.

(3) Protective laws which say you must not do this because it is likely to harm others.

The first kind of law cannot be justified. The second kind requires great care because legislators are apt to regard moral laxity as harmful even though there are only a few rare instances when one can hurt oneself by having sex. The third kind is defensible providing there are good reasons based on factual evidence.

There are three areas where a protective law may be justified:

(a) When sexual activities offend others who do not wish to be involved.

(b) When sexual activities are not the result of genuine consent.

(c) When sexual activities cause suffering, physical or psychological, to other people.

We do not see how the Sexual Containment Act can be said to come within any of these areas. This Act encourages a restrictive attitude, but we advocate a very frank and open attitude to sex, just as long as other people are not offended.

A protective law on obscenity would state that it is an offence for any person to expose to view explicit sexual material unless those who have been exposed to it demonstrate by their conduct that they do not object to it. Thus people who pay to see it, or join a club, or in some other way make a special effort should be free to enjoy it without interference. The law should only come into operation when people's susceptibilities are violated because they have stumbled upon this sexual material by mistake. The extent to which it is obscene, indecent or morally repugnant is irrelevant.

This means we must have a more sensible legal definition of privacy. At present the law permits the prosecution of people who, believing on reasonable grounds that they cannot be observed, are surprised by some chance encounter. What is even more ludicrous is that if a policeman goes to some trouble to find out what is going on, like joining a club that shows banned films or looking behind a hedge in the depths of the countryside, this is regarded as proof that the public might be offended. Furthermore mutual consent is not a defence under the existing law although it is strange that the organizers of nudist colonies are hardly ever prosecuted; there seem to be two standards, one for nudists, and another harsher one for lovers.

The public can be protected from annoyance by a fairly common sense definition of privacy. For example, an act is private when all the people present consent to it and when there is no reasonable cause to believe that it might be observed by others who might object to it.

The same definition should be applied to pornographic material. The question to ask is: Can those who object to pornography avoid it if they want to? If they can't, the display is illegal; if they can, then it doesn't matter whether it is hard or soft porn. So the law, which at present exerts all its energies towards stopping those who want pornography from enjoying it, should instead set out to protect those who do not want it.

To help those who do not like pornography, there should be some restrictions on displays and some warnings on the outsides of bookshops, cinemas, theatres and other places showing pornographic material. There should also be restrictions on unsolicited material coming through the post. Because TV programmes are less easily avoided, these would require special restrictions so as to avoid giving involuntary offence. But that is all. An adult should be allowed to read, see or hear what he wants to read, see and hear.

Sexual ignorance is often the direct cause of misery, and pornography can be a useful source of information. People learn about sex, not just from sex education classes and books, but from works of art, humour and entertainment.

The Japanese 'pillow books' are beautifully illustrated sex manuals, but in this country they would be legally banned as obscene. As long as pornography is illegal, it is inevitable that standards will be low; in this country erotica, which should be exciting and stimulating, is usually cheap and nasty. If the law was reformed, the presentation would be better, the customer would not be over-charged and the business would not be part of the criminal underworld with all that this implies in the way of protection rackets and police bribery.

Every member of the public has the right to be protected from over-explicit displays of sexual material and this should include hoardings, advertisements, window displays, unsolicited mailings and public entertainments which are, to him, offensive and annoying. But equally the individual has the right to expect protection against the police, press, busybodies, snoopers and informers who invade his privacy and question his right to carry on his sex life in his own way.

The one thing to be said in favour of the Sexual Containment Act is that it does not (ie cannot) distinguish between heterosexual and homosexual acts. Nevertheless other laws still on the statute book discriminate against homosexuals in the following ways:

1. The age of consent for heterosexuals is 16, but for homosexuals is 21.

2. The penalty for indecent assault on a male is a maximum of 10 years, but 2 years is the maximum for an indecent assault on a female.

3. The definition of privacy is more restrictive for homosexual acts.

4. It remains an offence for a third party to procure a homosexual act, even though such an act is now quite legal.

5. It is an offence for a man persistently to solicit another man for an immoral purpose, but no man has ever been prosecuted for soliciting a woman.

6. Local bye-laws are used against homosexuals in a way they are never used against heterosexuals.

None of these anomalies can be justified. As there is no discrimination between different forms of sexual behaviour in the Sexual Containment Act, no other law should prohibit conduct between persons of the same sex if it does not also prohibit similar conduct between people of the opposite sex.

In practice the Act indirectly encourages adolescents to have sexual intercourse before they are 16, the age when they are fitted with ORD. We would not worry about this if the adolescents were using contraceptives, but many young people who need advice about sexual matters are reluctant to ask for help when they know they are breaking the law by engaging in sexual activities below the age of consent.

The choice of 16 for the age of consent is quite arbitrary and there is no real biological justification for any particular age. Less than a hundred years ago the age of consent was 13. The Act takes no account of the fact that the age of puberty is much lower now than it was when it was decided, following a scandal about child prostitution in 1885, to make 16 the age of consent. There is no doubt that many girls and boys under that age are willing and eager to have sexual experience. The ability of teenagers to make sensible judgements and control their impulses depends on upbringing and education, not upon the law of the land.

The number of cases of rape has increased since the Act was passed because some people feel they are entitled to their full number of permitted orgasms, even if they cannot always find a willing partner. Rape carries a maximum penalty of life imprisonment and is regarded as a very serious offence. This means that the defence will go to considerable lengths to suggest that in reality the girl gave her consent. There are even suggestions that it is impossible for a girl to have sexual intercourse without her cooperation. Often the girl does not emerge from the case with her reputation unscathed.

Sex, above all things, should be a matter of choice. People should have it when they want it and should not be badgered into it when they don't want it. It should neither be restricted, nor be made obligatory. The Sexual Containment Act is an onerous restriction for many and an embarrassment for others who do not want to expend their PNO every quarter.

We know of many cases where these regulations have worked unfairly and capriciously, but we prefer to devote our limited space to criticizing the Act's inherent assumption that sex is basically evil and should be discouraged when it cannot be prevented. The authorities appear to believe that we shall inevitably become uncontrollably debauched and dissolute if they do not keep a firm control over our sexual desires. The inborn wickedness of mankind is a Christian myth which we reject absolutely. We believe that nearly all sex activities are not just harmless, but are positively beneficial.

Sex is a means of communicating delight between human beings. Not only does it give great pleasure, but it enables people to enjoy the pleasures of giving. It is the ideal form of communication, and often brings relief from loneliness. Anyone who believes human friendship is more important than material possessions would value a contented sex life above economic success or popular acclaim.

This does not mean to imply that sex and love must always go together. Sex can be entirely satisfying at a purely sensual level regardless of the depth of feeling involved. Hundreds of sexual acts occur every day between people who find one another attractive and between whom no other bond exists. Everyone knows that this happens to people who are neither indiscriminate nor mental and we fly in the face of all common sense when we try to pretend that the erotic desires of those who have sex without commitment are sordid or second rate. On the contrary, it is well known that these encounters are often very exciting and very enjoyable. The authorities who say that sexual intercourse should not be allowed unless both are in love are trying to deprive a lot of people of a lot of pleasure. As it happens, sex without commitment or without the pretence of love is an everyday occurrence, so it is not our actions that need changing but our ideology that requires revising. SIFS regards sexual intercourse as a continuation of friendship. We want people to put their talents to use, not in business or politics, but in bed.

The politicians who passed the Sexual Containment Act must think that sex is smutty, shameful, sinful and sinister. We think it is joyful and lovely, exciting and rewarding. The basic tenet of this society is that SEX IS FUN. Research results confirm this. In Schofield's study (*The Sexual Behaviour of Young Adults*, Allen Lane, 1973), over half of those questioned (57 per cent) said they had a sex problem and some of them mentioned more than one, but when they were asked if they found sex enjoyable, 95 per cent said they did. Despite all the attempts of the authorities to denigrate it, most people still managed to enjoy their sex lives.

The aim of SIFS is to reduce sexual problems and increase sexual happiness. Even for those who are worried, deprived or handicapped, sex helps them to find some peace of mind – an orgasm is a better tranquillizer than any pill. We aim to dispose of the myths and guilt feelings that surround sex, and to facilitate rather than frustrate our legitimate urge to have all the sex we want.

Politicians and people in authority think of sex as a very serious matter, never to be undertaken lightly, and only when certain conditions have been fulfilled. We say that sex is basically playful – little more than two people coming together to share mutual sensual pleasures. As often as not it is no more than an incident – very enjoyable but soon forgotten. The mistake is to take it all so seriously.

The fewer limitations there are on sex, the better for all of us. Why should we want to stop men, women, young or old from enjoying themselves? Adolescents reach puberty earlier and are physically healthier than ever before; it is not surprising that young people have sex on their minds almost as much as their elders. It is quite wrong to suppose that most people over 60 have lost interest in sex; there are many instances when a woman well past her menopause appears to take on a new lease of life because a man starts to take an interest in her.

We do not worry about who does what to whom and how. We are not concerned whether you are attracted to the same or the opposite sex or both. We do not think any part of the human body is shameful or sordid. We refuse to dictate which portals of entry are permissible.

We agree with the modern sociologists who define sexual deviance as a form of behaviour which is harmless in itself, but which provokes social hostility. Some hundreds of years earlier, Khojeh 'Omar Abu 'Othman, the Turkish author of *The Book of the Secret Laws of Love* advanced similar views:

> Most certainly (and Allah is All-Knowing) acts and ideas exist not as good or evil, right or wrong, natural or unnatural, but by reason of the nature of the prism through which our imagination considers and studies them. For example, we all know that there are some women who cannot experience an orgasm unless they are raped by their lovers, for these females respond rapidly to the most forceful thrusting and the most violent assaults. Allah accord them their desires.

SIFS is in favour of forceful thrusting for those who like it and gentle loving for those who prefer that. We are against those who insist that one form of sexual behaviour is superior to another. SIFS is also against words like lewd, lecherous, dissolute or debauched being used to describe people who just happen to like fucking.

But we don't want to sustain the illusion that sex is simply doing what comes naturally. There is much to be learnt. When things go wrong and sex goes sour, it is more likely to be due to ignorance than to wickedness. When a woman complains of a man's brutality, it is more likely to be clumsiness and poor technique. When a man complains about a woman's lack of response, it is more likely to be because she does not know how to express herself. When one partner complains that the other is inconsiderate, it is probably caused by embarrassment and by their inability to talk about appetites, erogenous zones and erotic possibilities.

Is sexual indulgence likely to be harmful for the individual or to others? Can too much sex be the cause of physical or mental ill-ness? Are the promiscuous unhappy and the lustful sad? We do not think so. The onus of proof is on those who wish to restrict sexual activities. The authorities point to the few who are over-indulgent, but almost any beneficial activity taken to excess becomes undesirable. It is absurd to use the compulsive collector of sexual conquests as an argument against making love, just as it would be wrong to take the 200 deaths a year from drowning as a reason for stopping millions from going for a swim. People who eat too much are not a convincing argument against good food.

The moralists quote VD and illegitimacy rates and cite the rare examples of impairment due to abortion, but there are always risks. It is a question of balancing them against the considerable ad-vantages of letting people decide for themselves how much sex they require. The major argument in favour of sex is that it gives many people an immense amount of pleasure. It is strange that the moralists so rarely mention the pleasurable aspects of sex. SIFS does not believe that it is either wrong or sinful to seek pleasure for its own sake.

Even the religious authorities now accept that people can have sex for pleasure and not just for reproduction. But they have not yet woken up to the fact that once you separate fun-sex from biological sex, many other strongly held beliefs lose their support. If it is agreed that the human genitals are not designed solely for procreation, then all sorts of non-coital activities can be enjoyed; for example, it is no longer rational to maintain that homosexual activities are unnatural; nor is there any logical objection to mas-turbation. If sex is for pleasure, then there is no longer any reason why two people should be committed to each other for life before they have sex together; in fact, they needn't even be in love, though it's probably more fun if they are – at least for the time being. Furthermore it is no longer sensible to uphold that idealized version of women who are more interested in motherhood than sex, because girls want sex for enjoyment just as much as men and the question of which partner has to bear the child becomes irrelevant when efficient contraceptives are being used. If sex does not have to be bound up with marriage and bringing up children, then it need not be taken so seriously, and we can take our sexual pleasures more casually and light-heartedly.

It is the element of compulsion that divides those who oppose

SIFS and those who support us. Our opponents want to compel
people to have less sex, but we don't want to force people to have
more sex. We should stop prohibiting people from having sex and
start helping people to find the sexual pleasures they do want and
can't get. Sex is for fun. We should have sex where, how, with
whom and when we want it.

Our opponents think our views are obscene and our policy
offensive. We are not offended by their views but we do think they
are intolerant. It is human intolerance that should be worrying us,
not the number of times we have an orgasm . . .